D0761029

Fly-Casting

FINESSE

Fly-Casting
FINESSE

A COMPLETE GUIDE TO IMPROVING ALL ASPECTS OF YOUR CASTING

JOHN L. FIELD

Skyhorse Publishing

For Gordy Hill

CONTENTS

FOREWORD

Wanting some help with his casting, an elderly gentleman from just up the road once came to my backyard for an evening lesson. We made some minor changes to his cast and he seemed happy with them. He called me excitedly a couple of weeks later to say that he had worn a path in his backyard along the measuring tape between his casting station and his targets. Speaking with a passion that belied his age, he said, "I've fallen in love with casting."

John Field has fallen in love with casting. When he writes here of how beautiful and inspiring good casting can be, he's talking about his own experience. And he's talking about mine.

My first memory of John is of seeing his explosive distance casts in Freeport, Maine. He had come to me for some training, but as I watched him easily blast casts past 90 feet, I realized that he had some gifts that I did not. I pointed him to the American Casting Association. His natural talent and lots of joyful practice led him to eventually head up the ACA and now to this book. It is a teacher's singular satisfaction to have planted a seed in a student and to see it grow as it has in John. It is most hearteningly true when the student surpasses the teacher.

In the summer of 2014, John and I were at a conclave of fellow casting wonks in Montana when he said, "We've gotten to know each other well around casting but we hardly know each other personally." Two months later, we were together on a slow river in Maine. His kids were in float tubes lashed to mine so John could freely work the shoreline. With their charming and intentional goofiness, the children made me forget that successfully guiding youngsters requires the skill set of the sainted. Meanwhile, John was, as we say, *tearing them up*. He hooked one after another in a fish fest that Maine smallmouth bass often provide. His joy at that experience reminded me that while casting in itself is beautiful and fun, beautiful casting is the way to beautiful fishing.

You will hear many names in this book. They make up the fabric of the vibrant fly-casting/fishing community in North America and beyond. John fondly honors every one of them by citing them herein, and he tacitly says something about the two sports in doing so. While many of us seek the near-monastic experience of losing ourselves in water, we can only plumb that water because of what our mentors and peers have patiently, even lovingly taught us. In naming his mentors and peers and their contributions, John personalizes his passion and embraces his unique community, our shared community.

May we all live long enough to remember when age or infirmity caused us to put down our fly-rod for the last time. What will endure then are memories of mountains and rivers and oceans and the fish we found in them. What will also endure are the personal bonds of teaching and learning, of casting and fishing together, and, if we are *very* blessed, the joy of floating with a friend's children down a slow-moving river in Maine.

—Macauley Lord

PREFACE

As President of the American Casting Association, I was scanning for any pearls among the spam in the general email inbox, when my eye caught something out of the ordinary. It was an email from Nick Lyons asking if we would be interested in producing a little casting book for Skyhorse Publishing, similar to a book on fishing knots the International Game Fish Association had written for them. Nick was consulting for his son Tony's new publishing company. I wrote an outline but Nick said it exceeded what he was looking for. He asked if we could meet.

Nick invited me out for lunch at a Spanish restaurant a few blocks from their office to mine for a book with a larger scope than originally requested. I had a great time sharing a huge paella with Nick and thoroughly enjoyed his wealth of stories and genteel manner. With his famous self-deprecating humor, he disarmed any apprehension I had. He informed me Tony would rather defer accepting new titles for the time being, but sometime in the future, he (Nick) would ask me to write my big book on casting.

The future crept up five years later when Nick crossed the room to greet me at Joan Wulff's eighty-fifth birthday gathering at the Catskill Fly Fishing Center and Museum in Livingston Manor, NY. I greeted Nick and was flattered he remembered me. I introduced my wife to my literary hero who published almost everything I ever enjoyed reading about fly fishing. In turn, he introduced us to Jay Cassell, Skyhorse's editorial director and former editor of *Field & Stream*. As we stood together, Nick told Jay that my initial outline was the most authoritative he'd seen on the subject of fly casting. I was floored and humbled. Nick asked me, are you ready to write the book we discussed? I couldn't refuse. After a wonderful afternoon celebrating Joan's birthday with distinguished guests such as Mari Lyons, John Randolph, Al Caucci, Ed Van Put, Floyd Franke, Ted Rogowski, and others, my wife and I went home and pondered how I was going to deliver on my new book commitment.

I had a couple of hurdles to jump before I could start writing in earnest, and I'm glad I waited. I performed some research in Europe and with Gordy Hill's Master Study Group before I signed a contract. I also had the good fortune to write two features published in *Fly Fisherman Magazine* during that time. The last hurdle was my lack of free time, since I was still president of the New York City chapter of Trout Unlimited and the ACA. My terms were to expire by 2013, and I was free and ready!

Long before I started writing the book, my friend Macauley Lord, IFFF Casting Board of Governors Emeritus and author, asked me some questions about my book plans to help get me on the right foot for the task. I shared my ideas about reconciling the major teaching and conceptual differences in the different camps of the casting world. Mac said, if you write this book for us (casting geeks), you might sell a few hundred copies. If you write it for fishermen, you might sell thousands. Mac's wisdom helped me define the audience and scope of this book. When I told Mac about my drawing plans to illustrate this book, he cautioned me not to rely on memory or imagination but to base the drawings on photographs. Photos capture what is really happening, not just what's in our minds. What a brilliant suggestion. Jim Krul at the Catskill Fly Fishing Center and Museum introduced me to Chris Theising, the photographer who made most of the images herein. Chris has been a delight to work with and also shared his beloved Neversink waters with me.

The title *Fly-Casting Finesse* was my idea but it probably influenced by the references to "finesse" used by some of my favorite fishing and casting authors, Rene Harrop, Joan Wulff, and Doug Swisher.[1] I also think the title has a little irony. Even when you're distance casting, you cannot use brute force: It corrupts form. Knowledge and consistency of proper form are what make a beautiful cast. A winning distance cast will look effortless when executed correctly, even though your ears tell you otherwise. Efficiency is very important, regardless of the line weight you're using, and it will be the small things that make a big difference. You will need finesse to present a fly and be successful.

Before introducing my book, I'd like to share my viewpoint on what fly-fishing should be. Some of you might even feel the same way. I've always accepted that a cast fly line should have enough energy stored in it to deliver a fly. In other words, you don't cast the fly and it pulls the line through the guides. This would only happen if the fly was heavily weighted and the fly line was short, underweight, or even mono, as Joe Humphrey sometimes used. I don't enjoy the process of Czech nymphing, casting "chuck 'n duck," split-shot or "slinky" rigs. In saltwater fly fishing, sinking lines and heavy flies are often a necessary evil, even to just reach many species or to cast in wind. Additionally, earning the bite of fish by sight-fishing is more challenging and rewarding than reading water or structure and catching unseen fish.

Many guides and fly fishing industry experts are now promoting the easiest, most productive ways to catch fish with a fly rod, or something resembling one. Some are trying to take casting out of our sport because it's too much bother for beginners to learn! I'm not among them. I welcome their disciples on the river with Tenkara or Euro-nymphing rods as much as I welcomed snowboarders on my favorite ski runs back in the eighties. I see nothing wrong with the bar being fairly high and I will assist anyone who wishes to attempt the hurdle. Half of the sport of fly fishing is the challenge of properly using the tackle. In the words of author Fred Mather, " . . . if you catch nothing, fly-casting is, like virtue, its own exceedingly great reward."[2]

My casting and teaching education and experience come from the International Federation of Fly Fishers and the American Casting Association and their generous members. I am an IFFF Master Certified Casting Instructor and have given many clinics, workshops, and hundreds of private lessons. I've logged forty-plus years of fly fishing with some of the best anglers and guides as mentors and companions. I've been a staff and freelance magazine contributor and traveled for four years with Larry Dahlberg, shooting and coproducing *The Hunt for Big Fish* on ESPN and other cable networks. I've also had the pleasure of fishing with Steve Rajeff in my home waters. I consider this book to be the culmination of my many years of research and fly casting.

[1] *Trout Hunter*, Rene Harrop, Pruett Publishing, 2003, p.106; *Fly Casting Techniques*, Lyons Press 1994, Joan Wulff, p.6; *Fly Fishing Strategy*, Lyons Press, Doug Swisher & Carl Richards, 1975, p. 53.

[2] *My Angling Friends*, Fred Mather, *Forest and Stream*, 1901, p.110.

INTRODUCTION

I don't know how many of you are expert casters, or have seen or known any, but if you are neither, I would like you to know how beautiful and inspiring good casting can be. Enthusiasts who have experienced the skills of top casters, revere them in a special way. Besides gaining admiration, being a top caster gives you the ability to solve presentation problems and catch fish where and when others dare not try. Being a good caster and a good angler usually goes hand in hand. Taking the first step toward good instruction is the first step toward better fishing and being an expert caster. It is not my intention for this book to replace the services of a casting instructor. I hope readers will discover casts and techniques in my book they were previously unaware of and seek out the best methods and instructors for learning them.

One purpose of this book is to share varying techniques from a wider perspective than I believe has been previously offered, in the hope that readers will increase their understanding and become more effective casters. In this book I try to identify styles and techniques and reasons they exist. I want anglers to know casting styles, techniques, and presentations that can be borrowed and adapted to deal with unique and difficult fishing situations. Most casting and presentation techniques taught today originated in the nineteenth century in Europe for salmon and trout angling. Since that time, anglers elsewhere have adapted these to the habits and habitat of their local fish species. There are gold nuggets in this book for any fly angler.

Many of you have bought this book, or are considering it, because you have arrived at a plateau in your casting and want to go to the next level, or even the pinnacle. That's the way I felt before I sought out the best instructors I could find. Through participating in the revelations of Gordy Hill's Master Study Group between IFFF Certified Instructors and invited guests, I realized most anglers assume what they were taught is the absolute truth and repeat it without questioning its validity. I have read the writing of some famous casting instructors who've expressed technically untrue ideas. The risk of this misinformation is a lack of understanding and the ability to solve problems. This book offers ways to qualify your instructors and make your own decisions.

The contents of this book will hopefully increase your casting distance and accuracy and put a few more presentational tools in your bag. It should help you relax and have less fatigue, develop better timing while increasing your awareness of the feeling of the rod, and accelerate it with less effort. A great caster casts with finesse that seems effortless, and when properly cast, a fly line is a thing of beauty. In the August 9, 2010, *New York Times* article *Where Anglers Rear Back and Let Fly*, James Card quoted me as saying, ". . . there's something intrinsic about casting that's kind of like hitting the sweet spot on a tennis racket or a nice golf drive . . . In fly casting, we like to see our loops in flight. We think they are graceful and beautiful. It just feels good." I like the pursuit of fish but I also like the activity of fly casting for them, and the lifetime of learning that mastery requires.

This book contains eight chapters with over one hundred drawings and photographs. I've provided many casting tutorials on how to identify and address faults. In this book, I believe for the first time, I've shown casting faults with stroboscopic photography. In Chapter 1, I discuss increasing the quality of practice and DIY versus personal instruction for learning casting or curing faults in the least time. This includes video analysis. Chapter 2 describes a loop and its variations in detail, so you can use casting mechanics to control loop shape for distance, wind, and special presentation casts. The stroboscopic photos of good and faulty casts are unique to this book. Chapter 3 is all about one-hand casting mechanics and worldwide adaptations in any plane and direction, including one-hand Spey casting. Chapter 4 starts with the fundamentals of accuracy, then covers casts for dead drifts, quick casts for saltwater, and casts for adverse situations. Chapter 5 has nine fresh- and saltwater presentation scenarios with recommended ways to fish them. Chapter 6 is an exhaustive resource on increasing casting distance. Chapter 7 covers all aspects of tackle design and choices. I offer my recommendations and rigging advice. Chapter 8 will help you understand the viewpoint and origin of international fly fishing organizations, clubs, and schools, so you can communicate more effectively and maybe adopt some new techniques.

I share lessons in this book from the generous members of the American Casting Association who are a repository of techniques handed down from old champions and tackle designers. Learning the old casting games has tangible benefits and offers great fundamentals for successful angling. The lessons I learned about distance, accuracy, and tackle design enriched all facets of my fly fishing. Many tournament casting techniques are not obvious to anglers or casting instructors, and I hope to share some of them with you in this volume.

After being the leader of the American Casting Association, I created its Casting History Committee so the origins of tackle and technique can be preserved in artifact, record, and literature. I've injected some history into this book to create perspective and to hopefully inspire innovation. It's comforting to know that right now, there is probably some-one out there casting in the dark with a glowing Lumilux line, trying to invent a new cast!

When I was growing up, I was a big fan of the book *The Sportsman's Notebook and Tap's Tips*, by H. G. Tapply. So, to pay homage to *Tap's Tips*, I've added Field Tips to this book. I've also included a glossary, cast graphics, and a list of learning resources. An e-book version of *Fly-Casting Finesse* will be available and will include casting tutorial video links.

I invite all yearning fly fishers to discover your fly-casting potential.

CHAPTER 1

MASTERING FLY CASTING

Most great casters have learned to cast automatically so they don't have to think about performing the casts. Their virtuosity enables them to invent a cast out of necessity and not even know it while they're doing it. They can get into the Zone, or the mindset, of a hunter and concentrate on insects, forage, currents, breezes, and fish. Their subconscious guides the rod. This book is targeted at anglers seeking to develop that level of skill. Getting there doesn't happen without time and effort.

In the 1990s, many anglers had what I call the *River Runs Through It* syndrome after viewing the Robert Redford movie based on Norman Maclean's book. When the movie starring Brad Pitt was big in the box office, inspired viewers bought fly outfits, yearning to experience what they felt watching the casting in the movie. Of course, the on-screen angler doubles for the difficult casts were two world-class casters and anglers: Jerry Siem, Sage Fly Rods designer, and Jason Borger, fishing and casting author. Lots of couples took big trips to the Rockies where the movie was set, unprepared for the angling challenges ahead. Unfortunately, many soon found attaining competency in dry fly angling would take too much practice for their busy lives and put away their shiny fly fishing outfits. Fly fishing is like golf or tennis, you must be dedicated to learn proper technique in order to develop skill. For these sports, it takes years of practice and experience to become really good. If you practice correctly, you'll gain performance and endurance, which is required for long fishing days. These can be enhanced with good physical conditioning or specific training.

Strength, endurance, speed, and coordination are required to excel at certain tasks in fly casting. Some of these abilities are genetic; others are learned or developed. It's like a magic formula for success when one person has the build and desire at an early age. Few have this gift but they still need the instruction and practice like everyone else. Everyone can advance their fly-casting skills if they are passionate, make good choices, and practice regularly. Starting to learn a sport at a young age is an advantage, but there is no better time to increase your dedication than now.

People who are serious about fly casting and fishing, like any sport or art, should seek qualified professionals with sound credentials and good recommendations. Stay away from egotistical self-serving experts who claim to have invented more than their share of techniques, and who insist there is only one right way to make a cast. Sometimes self-serving experts rename techniques or casts just to brand themselves for marketing purposes. Also, just because someone can cast well, doesn't mean they can teach it; teaching is a skill unto itself. A good instructor must be able to demonstrate and explain proper technique as well as identify and cure faults. They must also be able to adapt teaching methods for groups or individual needs.

This book is aimed at exploring casts, learning skills, and at helping break the bad habits that cause casting faults. Faults prevent accuracy, high line speed, and the execution of many casts. Every time you repeat a cast, whether it's bad or good, your nervous system learns how to repeat it again in the future. Most of us call this muscle memory. The more times you repeat a task, the more automatic it becomes. If you practice a cast several thousand times, you will develop what's called automaticity. This is the subconscious performing the task without having to think about the parts of the cast. If you're going to learn a cast, for goodness' sake, practice good form instead of bad. If you've learned bad habits, you can almost obliterate them through practicing the task correctly more times than you practiced it incorrectly. Faults still might pop-up from time to time, so vigilance is necessary. There has been a lot of research into the manner in which we learn. You can read some of these concepts from Daniel Coyle's book, *The Talent Code*, Bantam, 2009.

The best way for our brain to learn physical tasks is to break them into the smallest possible steps and learn them by rote. Slowing down a task is also a way for the brain to absorb the technique more thoroughly. After you can do the task slowly with good form, you can practice it at a faster speed, until you can perform it at normal speed and still maintain good form. This works well for pantomiming and learning how to do the double haul. It helps to make the practice efficient and enjoyable. The more deeply we concentrate on practicing without distraction, the better we learn. This concept is the same whether you're learning accuracy casting, or playing a musical instrument.

Set reasonable long-term objectives but start at a beginning point, then increase the goals each session when you achieve them. For example, cast 60 feet without faults and increase the goal by a couple feet each session. Only advance to the next task when you master the current one. This takes time and repetitious practice. If your form deteriorates during practice, stop immediately and correct it or return to the task when you're fresh. Ideally, it's best to stop before that point, when you've finished your repetitions or session with good form. Intense desire and ambition are two requisites for successful learning. To begin, you should make a plan toward your goal then follow it all the way.

METHODS OF LEARNING: VERIFYING RESULTS

You can work on your casting alone, with a mentor, an instructor, a school, or a combination. You should be able to find casting coaches and instructors almost all over the world. You can find them through fly shops, clubs, and organizations. The Internet has hundreds of casting videos, blogs, and apps for do-it-yourselfers. One problem with the Internet is the lack of qualification of the content creator. Anyone can be a self-proclaimed authority. Only use sources and instructors whose credentials or names you recognize and whose materials make sense to you. The last chapter of this book is about some of the different casting schools and their unique viewpoints. Collaborating with people who are moving up in their learning curve can be another positive influence in the learning process for both parties. You can take turns checking your casts and sharing what you've learned. This collaboration could be online and in person.

Visual verification is one of the most important tools in learning to cast well. Seeing what's going on will help identify faults and flaws. Ask someone with experience to observe your casts, or video record yourself and analyze the footage. If an instructor or experienced friend spots a fault, have them record it on video for you to see. Faults are more easily believed and understood if seen by the caster, than described by someone else.

Someone who knows what to look for can examine video at a later time or shared online if they are not present when you're casting. With today's technology, you can even upload your video and share the link with a coach three thousand miles away and they can add analysis for you to see.

Today's apps can help by visualizing your casts.

The current hardware and software solutions for video analysis are devices like the Apple iPad or Android tablets and apps such as UberSense and Coach's Eye. I use Coach's Eye to compare two casters or a before and after during side-by-side video playback. The video scroll wheel lets you clearly show action back and forth and at any speed or cue it to an exact spot. The apps enable you to draw on the screen with your finger and even measure angles. You can use a bracket and tripod or clamp or your observer can handhold the tablet for capturing the casts. If the screen is too small or the sun is too bright, you can use a video display or wide screen TV indoors.

Most casting instructors use an athletic field or a park lawn for teaching. A lawn gives the instructor control of some important elements. The instructor can pick and change the set-up in relation to wind and sun and can also set up lines, markers, and targets. On a field, the instructor can walk around the caster and check tracking and important loop characteristics. The solid green grass also provides a good background for a method of learning called horizontal or ground casting. Even though this technique is used for beginners, I think it is helpful when practicing more advanced casts like low-sidearm, non-dominant hand casting, the cross-body cast, and more. Unfortunately, grass is more difficult when learning waterborne casts like roll and Spey casts.

Joan Wulff showed me her horizontal casting set-up and included it in her book update, *Joan Wulff's New Fly Casting Techniques*, pp 45–46. Her late head instructor and dear friend Floyd Franke used a wooden form lying on the ground with four sticks representing different rod arcs. The rod arc is the change of angle of the rod butt from stop to stop. I set up this drill with four fluorescent orange mini sport cones and place three in a line fifty feet long; one in

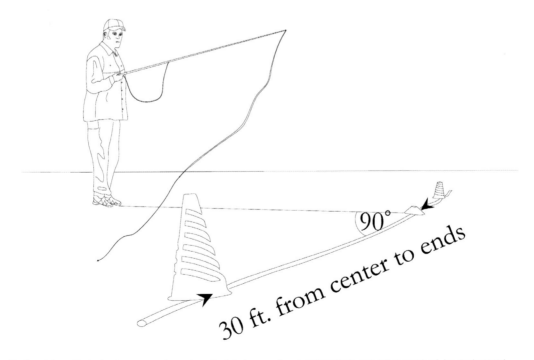

Horizontal casting, also known as ground casting, helps you learn better than any other method, by seeing and breaking down the parts of a cast.

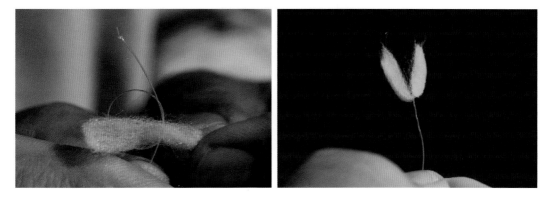

Using a bright yarn fly helps you see where your casts land and gives enough drag so you can see the leader better during practice.

the middle and one at each end. The fourth cone should be placed your rod's length away from the middle cone. Now standing with both feet behind the fourth cone and your rod held horizontally in front of you with 25 feet of line and leader extended, cast from end cone to end cone. If you let the fly land, it should land on the line or on a cone.

The real object is to illustrate the relationship between the rod arc, a quick rod stop, and loop width; to cast with the rod tip moving over the imaginary straight line between the cones by using the optimal stroke with the correct balance between translation and rotation. Translation is the horizontal movement of the rod made in the direction of the cast, without a change rod arc. If your trajectory is wavering or your loops aren't the same on your back and forward casts, follow a horizontal fence or roofline with your rod tip to practice a straight, smooth stroke.

FIELD TIP

The quickest way to make a practice fly is to use a little fluorescent Glo-bug yarn tied in the middle with a jammed overhand knot and doubled back. I like a dark color on snow and chartreuse for the lawn.

DIAGNOSING AND CURING FLAWS

Regardless of what type of cast you are trying to perform and what casting style you prefer, use good mechanical fundamentals to achieve efficient and effortless casts. Faults prevent a caster from having good, efficient loops, and even cause unnecessary fatigue. Good fundamental form will give a caster control over loop size and shape and provide control over accuracy and distance.

Good casters and instructors can identify faults by looking at what the line does. We examine loop shape, tracking, line tension, speed and trajectory, etc. We also listen to sounds made by the rod and line, which are indications of speed and friction. Then, diagnosing why the problem in the line is occurring is a matter of watching the rod in action and which body movements cause it. Video will help you see for yourself. Faults are usually in the stroke or haul mechanics and also in timing. To cure the problem, you change the fault caused by the body. This will remedy the fault in the rod-tip path, and that will cure the fault in the line. Bruce Richards was first to detail this process and called it the "Six-Step Approach to Casting Faults and Cures" which was published in the Spring 1999 issue of IFFF's *The Loop Newsletter*. Bruce Richards was the chief line designer for Scientific Anglers for many years until his retirement and returned as a consultant after Orvis purchased it from 3M in 2013. Bruce wrote the book *Modern Fly Line* (1994) and codeveloped the Casting Analyzer. It's best to learn good form when you begin a new skill because bad habits are hard to break. Fortunately, you can even correct old problems with the help of a coach and some casting maintenance. I've included fault identification and cures in each of the tutorials on technique in this book.

DRILLS AND MAINTENANCE

If you or your instructor have diagnosed one or more casting faults in your casting, you need to practice drills to overcome them. Try to practice where the experience simulates the conditions in which you will be fishing. There is a difference between practicing on water versus land, and still water versus running water. Water tension is a good thing to have if you're practicing roll casts or Spey casts. It also has an affect on loading when practicing pick-ups. After learning the presentation casts for running water on the lawn, also try them on water with a yarn fly before going fishing. The current affects the layout and shape of the line as you present it and changes it continuously as it travels downstream.

The catch cast helps deliver the fly and leader to hand in an instant, with a snap.

Don't forget to check the results every day, once a week, or whenever you suspect something isn't right. Use a qualified friend to observe, a video camera, or a casting instructor. If your fault returns, resume the same drills or consult an instructor or books for additional drills. A good instructor should have many different tools in his toolbox to deal with different levels of fault severity and persistence. Also, everyone absorbs information in different ways and instructors have to offer teaching options for the variances in human beings.

Practicing casting skills year-round will help your casting become more automatic. I like casting on snow with a fluorescent line because its visibility is enhanced and snow keeps the line clean. When you can't cast outdoors, you can use indoor practice rods to help your subconscious remember how to cast. After learning good consistent form and the ability to form good loops, you will be ready to refine them and move on to accuracy and distance technique.

FIELD TIP

The catch cast is used to quickly bring the fly to hand to check it or the leader or make changes. Facing the line on the water, make a lift of the rod-tip head high then snap the tip down to the water and the line will form a loop and fly toward you. As the loop opens, reach out and catch the end of the leader.

CHAPTER 2

THE LOOP & THE ROD

The loop is the Holy Grail of fly casting. When a loop is well formed, it is a graceful inspiration, full of paradox. It seems to be a living thing, rising, flying fast, or slowly hanging in the sky, undergoing a metamorphosis of shapes. A loop is the shape of a line in the air as a result of a cast made with an acceleration ending in a stop. The loop is comprised of three parts. The front of the loop is aptly called the point. The line from the rod tip to the point of the loop is called the rod leg of the loop. The portion from the point, to the leader, is the fly leg of the loop. The more parallel these legs are, the more aerodynamic the loop will be. If the fly leg sticks out, it's like sticking your arm out while skiing down a mountain.

Until the 1940s the loop was called a bow and described as either a "tight" bow or a "wide" bow. A loop can be formed with various characteristics, but tightness is the one many of us spend our lives pursuing. A loop of three feet between the fly and rod leg is considered tight. The tight loop is more efficient for defeating wind than a wide loop. When combined with high line speed, parallel legs, the right trajectory, and direction, a tight loop will travel the greatest distance.

If you want to learn how to control the tightness and shape of the loop, it is important to understand how and when the loop is formed. The bow-and-arrow cast shows us we don't need to make a stroke to form a loop and the stop in that case is just the resistance of the hand holding the handle still (see Bow-and-Arrow Cast p. 77) A hand-cast shows us you don't even need a rod to form a loop. But a specific sequence of actions does need to occur to produce a good loop in overhead casts.

Our backcast starts with a taut line and a low rod tip position. If casting on water, lifting the line breaks water tension and on grass, overcomes the friction and starts to load the rod, or bend it. You must continue accelerating the rod with the stroke of the rod hand on a given trajectory and load the rod. To properly perform the cast,

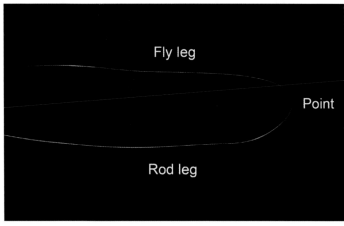

Different parts of the stroke affect different parts of the loop. The behavior of different parts of the loop affects the quality of the cast.

the acceleration must be smooth and continuous during the stroke or an improper bend in the rod tip will misdirect the line. The rod-tip path can vary and produce poor loops but a straight path is crucial to forming an efficient loop shape. The caster begins the stop sequence by decelerating the rod and as a result, the energy loaded into the bend of the rod unloads, transferring itself to the line and the line overtakes the rod tip. It is at this point the loop is formed above the rod tip. The caster waits for the unrolling of the loop before starting the forward cast.

After the rod unloads, it passes through a cycle of vibra-

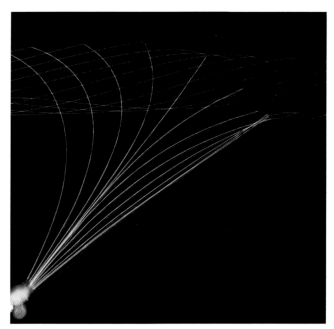

In this forward cast, the rod unloads and straightens, then bends in the casting direction and back. This is the process of counterflex and rebound.

tions, straightening and flexing until it rests or is cast again. When the rod bends past straight in the casting direction, the motion is called counterflex. After counterflex, the rod tip returns back to a straight position. This straightening is called rebound.

During this rebound, the loop is unrolling and before it falls, the caster reverses casting direction by starting the forward stroke with a forward acceleration of the rod hand which finishes the rod loading at the end of the stroke. The stroke is ended by the intentional muscle contraction in the arm, wrist, hand, and shoulder or when the casting arm and other skeletal movement are fully extended at the completion of the delivery stroke. On the forward cast, the rod moves through a similar cycle as on the backcast but I'm about to examine a forward delivery cast, with emphasis on loop creation.

The shape of the delivered loop is created by the combination of a straight rod-tip path, the timing and duration of the stop sequence and line release, and their relation to the oncoming line. Bill Gammill, International Federation of Fly Fishers Casting Board of Governors member and author of *The Essentials of Fly Casting*, Federation of Fly Fishers, 1993, and others have taught us to make the rod tip travel in a "straight line" path to form an efficient loop. This concept can help in rudimentary learning but we know it is not perfectly accurate. In a good cast the tip path is almost straight or has straight segments, as shown in photographs.

The rod tip bends downward during deceleration and out of the way of the oncoming line. If in reality the path would be perfectly straight, the line would often collide with itself and the rod tip. The same would be true if we used a perfectly vertical rod casting position. The cast is made above the rod tip and gravity lowers its flight. At minimum, a slight outward rod tilt, depending on wind direction, helps prevent midair collisions.

During a properly made overhead cast, the loop, including the fly leg, should propagate in the same plane the rod travels, due to the

The path of the rod tip is critical because it determines the loop shape and size. When the path is straight, it is called SLP, Straight Line Path.

centrifugal force of the rotational path of the rod tip. Scientists who've studied the cast even call a good loop a "planar loop." Therefore the fly leg will be directly above the rod leg when casting with the rod plane is vertical. When you tilt the angle of the casting plane, the effects of gravity will make the fly leg twist downward. We use these dynamics to our advantage when making the pendulum or upside-down-loop cast (see p. 76).

For years, casters, anglers, and casting educators have been trying to uncover the secrets of loop formation and stroke mechanics in order to perfect casting and teaching technique. Several individuals in conjunction with educational and private labs have used motion capture (or Mo-Cap) studies to freeze elements and relationships in a cast that are too fast or complex to see in real time. Some investigators have broken down the cast into a sequence in order to help discover the instant of loop formation and its variables. The rod bend and tip position in relation to loop formation and stroke have been frozen into graphics and photos for analysis. This has had a profound effect on our discovery and understanding. In the following illustration

Rod Dynamics During Forward Cast

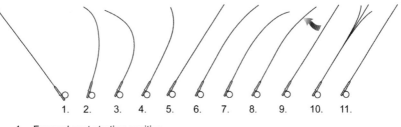

1.   2.   3.   4.   5.   6.   7.   8.   9.   10.   11.

1. Forward cast starting position
2. Stroke begins and accelerates rod and line
3. Maximum rod load (bend.) MRL
4. The stop sequence starts. Rod moves fastest as it straightens.
5. Rod moves through its first straight position (called, RSP 1).
        The loop begins to form as the fly line overtakes the rod tip.
6. The rod bends in the direction of the cast. This is called counterflex.
7. Point of maximum counterflex. (called MCF).
8. Now, the rod tip starts to spring back. This is called rebound.
9. The rod straightens for the second time, (called RSP 2).
10. The rod vibrates
11. The rod rests at the final straight position (called RSP3).

Understanding the dynamics of the rod and line can help a caster increase casting ability and cure faults. This was recreated from the original by Gordy Hill and used with his permission.

("Rod Dynamics During Forward Cast"), note the progression from the loaded rod to MRL to the "stop" sequence from deceleration to RSP, RSP 1-loop formation and launch, and the continuation of rod movement through counterflex, MCF, and then the change in rod tip direction and rebound.

LOOP SHAPE

Beyond making tight loops to reduce drag, the ultimate refinement in streamlining is loop sharpening and line damping. In our collective quest for perfection, the first questions are: When is the loop born? and How can we influence its shape? Bruce Richards has had extensive experience working with his coinvention, the Casting Analyzer, that uses an angular rate gyro on the rod butt and a palm pilot:

> If we want to define when loops actually form, I'd vote for it being when fly leg speed first becomes higher than tip speed. In most normal casts this will happen right at RSP. The rod tip continues to accelerate to RSP, rapidly decelerates after that, but the fly leg does not. How quickly the rod decelerates, and how briefly the stop is made has an impact on loop size and shape also. Quick deceleration means there is less rotation during the stop, which keeps the rod tip higher, which raises the bottom (rod) leg. How complete the stop is does the same thing. In most casts the caster doesn't stop the rod completely, but slows it to 30–50 deg/sec of rotation (as measured by the Casting Analyzer).

Bruce Richards also adds, "The 'stop,' which is simply rod deceleration, must be rapid. A very fast stop keeps the rod tip high, maintaining top (fly) leg straightness. A slow stop results in a curving tip path and a curved top leg where it attaches to the loop front; much less efficient." Bruce has been able to identify how to replicate good casts. He describes some requirements:

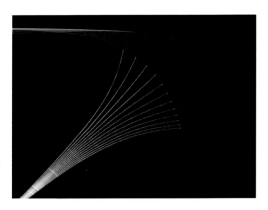

The loop forms just after RSP-1 when the line overtakes the speed of the rod tip.

All wedge loop casts are made with very constant angular rotation. This makes sense, as these loops must have very straight top legs; that is what leads to the tight top radius that is the hallmark of wedge loops. If you envision a loop with an upward curving top leg you can quickly see that it will not have a nice top pointed wedge. The thing that makes a very straight top leg is a very straight tip path leading to RSP, and that comes with very constant acceleration.

What happens after RSP will determine how the loop front will look initially as it leaves the rod. Usually there will be significant rebound, which will round the loop and make it look less pointed than it will eventually become. As the loop progresses forward, tension between the loop front and rod tip will lift and straighten the bottom leg, which accentuates the true wedge shape of the loop.

Casting with good tracking and a straight-line rod-tip path are prerequisites to form a tight loop with parallel legs. A loop with a sharp point is the most aerodynamic. Using constant acceleration and a brief stop helps loop sharpness and tightness. Paul Arden, top international casting instructor, operator of the casting website and tackle brand Sexyloops, summarizes some of the dynamics of producing a tight loop:

> The rod tip is traveling at its fastest just before RSP. As we know, everything up to RSP during the line acceleration forms the top/fly leg of the loop and everything after RSP to counterflex forms the bottom, or rod leg. The closer to RSP the line is released, the tighter the loop will be . . . The sharpness of the point as I understand it, is the difference in tension between the two legs.

Gordy Hill also shares a tip from a fishing friend: "I make that sharp 'chiseled' loop the way Steve Rajeff once taught me . . . by making a very brief forward and upward thrust with the rod tip so close to the point of unloading that I can't tell if it is actually AT that point or at RSP 1."

The way to control loop shape is to choose the proper rod and line combination and learn good stroke and damping techniques. I will address these shortly.

Steve Rajeff, world casting champ and senior rod designer for G.Loomis, at the IGFA/ACA event in 2010. He said, when he was learning to cast, his distance really took off when he learned how to make a positive rod stop. Photo credit: John Field

CHAPTER 3

CASTING MECHANICS AND ADAPTATION

Overhead casts refer to casts that create a rolling and unrolling loop made in the air and not casts that are waterborne or anchored in the water. Roll cast and Spey casts are water-anchored and their loops are made under the rod tip. Instead of only using the weight of the unrolled line in the air to load the rod, water-anchored casts use the effective part of the D-loop and line end in the air plus the resistance caused by water tension. In most fishing situations, overhead casts are superior to water-anchored casts for achieving maximum casting distance but require the space for the extended line and leader to unroll. Backcasts and forward casts are considered two separate casts, even if linked together in a sequence, like a pick-up and laydown. The fundamental overhead cast is a straight-line cast, where the backcast and forward cast should be opposed 180 degrees. In the absence of wind, the casting strokes and acceleration of the rod should be the symmetrical and the resulting loops should be identical. As I'll cover later however, there are certain circumstances in advanced casting that combine different, asymmetrical casts.

The goal in overhead casting is to master accuracy, distance, casting in wind, changes of casting direction, and presentation casts. Another important goal is to cast efficiently without injury or excessive fatigue. Since this is an advanced casting book, I'm going to describe and analyze the basic cast, offer some refinements, and then delve into specific areas of application. Once you master the fundamentals, you are able to learn more difficult casts and even combine them to

Moving your body in the direction of the cast can increase line speed and distance.

execute a fishing strategy. The parts of the cast and how well they interact in a seamless, smooth sequence have a profound effect on performance and efficiency. I've included a glossary of terms and definitions that I use and have been unofficially accepted by the IFFF at an earlier point in time, and many are still used. If you've been taught other terms for the parts of the cast, at least you can correlate them to my descriptions and know my intent.

STANCE

Good casting is about control and it starts with the feet. A practical and consistent casting stance is equally important to accurate casting as it is to distance casting. It can help stability, aiming, weight transfer, and rotation. Weight transfer is a movement of the body toward the direction of the cast that helps accelerate the arms and the rod in making a cast. It is also an addition to the total casting arc. Different stances set the limits for the range of body movement and help prevent excessive movement. Weight transfer is essential in using heavy tackle, overcoming wind, and increasing casting distance. There are times when lower body movement will scare fish and other situations when it won't. When wading in current, you don't have much choice. You pretty much have to stand sideways to the flow to deflect water and reduce drag. You might be limited only to upper body and trunk movement. When you can move, stance will help your accuracy.

I've taken notice of the body stance and movement of anglers and tournament casters and concluded that stance is highly individual. Chris Korich, ACA Hall of Famer and "Casting Jedi" of the Oakland Casting Club, instructed me to point the foot on my casting side toward the target for good accuracy. He said, it's just like a basketball player making a free throw. Keeping this foot forward helps align the body with the target. It can also act as a body

A closed stance is when the lineup of your feet is perpendicular to the casting direction. An open stance is when one foot is forward. An open stance is best for weight transfer.

block in distance casting since it helps prevent unwanted upper torso rotation. Most anglers keep the opposite foot forward since that is the preferred distance stance and easiest to perform any weight transfer. Fly-casting stances are described in several ways.

In a square stance, the hips and feet are in a perpendicular line to the target and the front of your body faces the casting direction. In this position, both feet can be as wide apart as shoulder width. Most people also call this foot position a closed stance. If you drop one foot back, it's an open stance. An open stance puts the feet on an imaginary line parallel to or at an angle to the target. As I mentioned earlier, when anglers wade in current, they stand sideways with one hip into the flow to decrease drag. When you are on land, a dock, or on a vessel, you aren't as limited in regard to stance. Almost all tournament distance casters and saltwater anglers use the open stance.

GRIPS

Different ways of gripping the rod can work better with different types of casts because they limit or permit certain ranges of movement or reinforce stiffness. Some people adopt one grip for life and others use two or more grips, depending on the situation. There are three major grips.

The first and most traditional is the "thumb-on-top" grip. In this grip, the heel of the hand should be placed on top of the handle. Some proponents, such as Joan Wulff, say it is the strongest grip for distance casts.

Second is called the V-grip (see photo) or as Chris Korich calls it, the natural grip, and Mel Krieger called the extended finger grip. Mel was a Golden Gate Angling and Casting Club legend, author, and FFF leader who mentored many casters. The handle is held in the joints of fingers 2-5 and the palm, and rests between the thumb and index fingers. The wrist is slightly pronated from the thumb-on-top grip. I learned this grip from ACA casters who use it for both accuracy and distance casts. In our tournament events, wrist strength is as important for straight lay-downs in accuracy events as it is for distance. A side wind tries to move the rod and line off target and you should compensate for this with your arm and wrist.

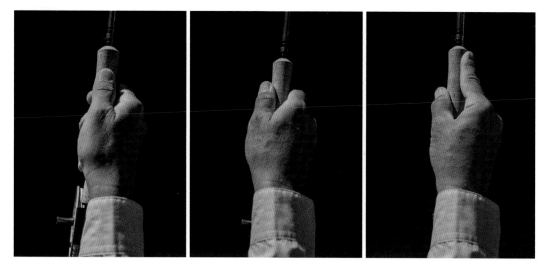

Thumb-on-top grip (left), V-grip (middle), and Three-point grip, or Distal grip (right).

According to Dr. Gary Eaton, D.O. and IFFF Master Certified Instructor, the V-grip is theoretically the strongest grip for distance casting but he doubts anyone uses it all the time, nor would they want to. He believes it could lead to connective tissue injury. He says, like himself, good casters rotate between the V-grip and thumb-on-top during casts without even realizing it.

The third is the "distal" or "three point grip," (see photo) which is a modification of the V-grip. The index finger is extended up the handle. This grip helps hold the rod more rigidly for good aiming alignment. Author and fly-fishing expert, Gary Borger, told me recently it is the strongest grip when the tip of the index finger is slipped slightly rearward to tension the finger like a leaf spring. I asked him why Steve Rajeff and other ACA and ICSF distance casters don't use it and he said they were taught the other way! The distal grip is Gary's son Jason Borger's and Fly Fishing U.S. National Champion George Daniels's preferred grip. The late Lee Wulff of Lew Beach, NY, and Hans Gebetsroither of Austria, father of the "Belgian Cast," also used this grip. You can also feel vibrations better with the index fingertip on the blank but I believe this grip is a disadvantage for heavy outfits or long casts.

Whether you use one grip over another is a matter of personal preference. I personally think the V-grip has no limitations and can be changed into the distal grip just by extending the index finger. Whichever grip you use, don't grip the rod too tightly. If you're gripping lightly, shock waves in the rod dissipate but if you're gripping too tightly, the rod will bounce, forming sine waves that travel down the fly line. The same applies to holding a bow in target archery. Lightly gripping a bow handle lets the limbs dissipate vibration with minimal adverse affect on arrow flight.

When you're accelerating the fly rod, squeeze the grip and load the rod. When you stop your rod and the rod's stored energy unloads into the line, relax your grip during the pause and let the rod absorb its movement without feedback to the line. Joan Wulff says tension should only be used during the power snap. The power snap is Joan's term for the fast acceleration of the stroke that ends with a stop.

THE STROKE AND ROD LOADING

In sports that use a racquet, bat, club, or rod, the motion with the hand gripping the handle is called the stroke. The casting stroke is the path of the rod hand executing either a forward cast or backcast. In fly fishing, the stroke and the movement of the rod and the line are linked together. The rod acts partly as a spring and partly as a lever. A loaded rod is a bent rod and is like a bent spring or limbs of a bow. You load a rod in two ways. The first is to bend the rod by accelerating it with the rod hand against a resistance of the weight of the line and the rod in the air, or additionally, the resistance of water or other surfaces. Secondly, you can load a rod by resisting with the rod hand and pulling line with the line hand as in the bow-and-arrow cast (see p. 77). Once again, forward and backcasts should be considered two separate casts. When casting a given distance without wind resistance, the acceleration of the stroke should be the same for a backcast as for the forward cast.

To form a reasonably well-formed loop, the rod must be loaded by the acceleration of the stroke and stopped close to the point of unloading, or where the rod first straightens. Unloading is also the transfer of energy from the rod to the line. The stroke of a fly rod should be made smoothly, with constant acceleration, or it will affect the quality of the cast. The best way to understand the relationship between loading and the stroke is by following what the rod tip does during a cast. If you call the

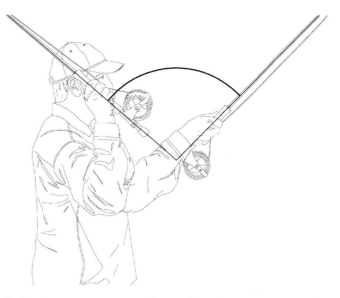

Rod arc is important because it is one of the biggest determinants of loop size.

rod tip point A and the butt cap point B, the distance directly between them is longest when the rod is straight. When you load, or bend the rod, this cord length, or distance, shortens. The dynamics of the changes in this length and the path the hand takes will determine the path of the rod tip during the cast. When a cast of a given length is made with the goal of making a tight loop, the caster should match the stroke and acceleration to the action of the rod in relation to the load, in order to make the straightest possible path of the rod tip. This is one of the first requirements in order to cast a tight loop.

As mentioned earlier, rod arc is the change in angle of the rod butt between the stops used to make two consecutive strokes. Rod arc is the result of the stroke, body movement, and loading and unloading. Because of translation, the bottom end of the rod doesn't rotate around a fixed point like the fixed point of a protractor. Instead, the rod travels in a shape resembling an annular sector. The whole body should work together to provide a stable path for accelerating the rod and casting the line.

When performing a straight-line cast, the rod should track through the air in

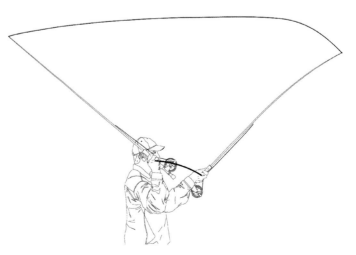

This shape comparison validates the idea that the rod doesn't rotate around a fixed center and thus SLP (Straight Line Path) requires translation, as shown in the next illustration.

one plane from beginning to end. The combination of stroke, body movement, and hauling to a small degree, work together to load a rod against the line and rod weight and all types of resistance and friction. Translation and rotation, or angular motion of the rod butt, are the two major movements in a cast. Translation adds some acceleration as can be evidenced by the feat of hand casting a line 90 feet without a rod. Ellis Newman, who taught me how to cast when I was seven, demonstrated this at shows. The stroke and body motion in the hand cast is purely translation.

The rotation of the rod butt is created by the various joints in our bodies from our ankles, spine, arms, and lastly to the wrist of the rod hand. The major rotation occurs in the shoulder, elbow, and wrist joints. Proper rotation caused by the stroke and by loading, multiplies the tip speed and contributes most to high line-speed. The flexor and extensor muscles of the arms and wrist provide the force for these movements. Not only do the arms and shoulders provide acceleration but they also stabilize the rod for straight tracking or casting a variety of rod paths and for making adjustments for wind. If you must repeat hundreds of casts a day on the water or in a tournament, use the largest muscles possible. This applies even in performing the smallest casts. Using the shoulders and core will stabilize the rod plane and reduces the fatigue of smaller muscles. This is why good casters don't rely on the wrist for doing most casting. The wrist is used in conjunction with bigger muscles and large joint rotation. These movements together combine to make the desired rod arc in order to make a tight loop. The way to get the most from your wrist is to cock it before a stroke requiring a greater range of movement. For example, to get a good line-lift off the water, the wrist should be straight during rod loading and snapped slightly past straight during the last few inches of the backcast. It is now cocked and loaded for the forward cast.

Efficient false casting and double-hauling are essential to creating a good loop and launching a long cast. If you are only casting 40 feet of line, use a medium-length stroke. When you're making a long delivery cast, use a longer stroke to enable the rod tip to load incrementally in a relatively straight-line path. This concurs with Bill Gammill's teaching: "The longer the cast; the longer the stroke." Translation also increases the length of the straight-line path of the rod tip as illustrated in *Casting and Fishing the Artificial Fly,* John W. Ball, Caxton Printers Ltd., 1972, p. 63 (Fig. 8) "Movement of Casting Hand." John Ball shows the addition of horizontal hand motion and states on page 62, " . . . this method can add many feet to your longest cast."

This is why I teach a short foundation stroke for efficiency and good tracking and when I see the student is ready, I teach adjustable stroke length and other techniques. This also means adding more translation. By increasing the stroke length, you also decrease the angle between the rod tip and the line. A long stroke is more like pulling a rope and less like prying with a lever. It can make longer casts easier for many people. Also, when distance casting, a softer rod requires a longer stroke to maintain a straight rod-tip path than one with a stiffer action.

The backcast is usually more difficult than the forward casts for most casters to master. That's because of physical and visual differences between them. The relative difficulty also depends on your casting style. The higher the stroke, the more upper shoulder muscles are involved, and the lower the stroke, the more the lower shoulder are used. Both the back and forward casts use the

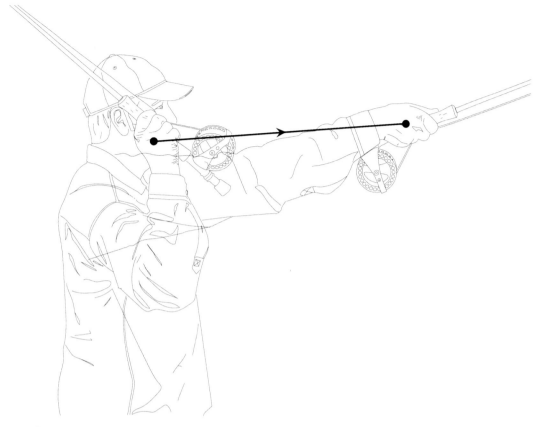

Translation helps match the amount of acceleration to rod loading to achieve SLP.

forearms and wrist. The biceps and rear shoulder muscles are the main ones used in the pulling motion of the backcast stroke. The forward cast uses more of the triceps and deltoids. The caster can easily watch the forward cast. Watching what's going on behind is more difficult. The tendency when watching the backcast is to turn and rotate the neck and shoulders and cause tracking problems. Try to only turn your neck when watching the backcast. The brim of a hat should not unnecessarily limit one's field of view. Seeing the line helps you cast better.

Assuming a backcast is made with good tracking, the two main determinants of a good backcast are loop size and speed and trajectory. The path the rod hand takes and where you

The 180-degree principle increases cast efficiency and proper loop formation.

stop the rod will determine the initial trajectory. The loop size and shape will be determined by where and how abruptly the rod is decelerated. The 180-degree principle should be followed to pull the line in the most direct route and to prevent various collisions.

CASTING STROKE STYLES

> But you can't do a thing unless you can cast: it's that fundamental. And now and then, watching one of the masters in motion, I had an itch to become truly dazzling with the tool . . . But they all did it so differently . . . Each had, what we call in stuffy English departments, a style of his or her own. *Style l'homme.*
>
> —Nick Lyons, *Full Creel* (2000)

As I always say, "Different strokes for different folks." There are two major one-hand fly casting stroke styles used today throughout the world. These styles can be used to make straight line and oval and elliptical casts. There are practical reasons for the evolution of different styles and they have become part of fly-fishing culture. These styles are often handed down or taught without being questioned. Quick lessons on the lawn seldom include mechanical analysis and alternative techniques. You're in charge of your fly-casting advancement and if the process of learning feels right and natural, you'll learn more successfully. Fly casters should experiment a little and use a style that works for them as a default or as options for specific situations. Styles can even be blended together. The famous casting instructor Al Kyte is given the attribution for the phrase, "Style is self-optimization."

The first stroke style I'll describe is the low side-arm stroke, sometimes called the saltwater style or Eastern style. It is used and taught by many, including Lefty Kreh who is one of the pioneers of saltwater fly fishing. He tells his students to keep their "elbow on the shelf" in a hori-zontal motion while casting. It is usually performed with a rod angle around 45 degrees with a thumb-on-top grip. This helps prevent the fly from hitting the caster in moderate winds. The rod hand reaches rearward on the backcast when attempting long casts, even with stiff rods. Lefty's long time friend Gordy Hill says Lefty's style is, " . . . a modified ellip-tical cast in which the backcast and forward casts are in a slightly different rod plane. The backcast with a more horizontal rod plane; the forward cast in a more off-vertical plane."

This style uses a great amount of stroke-length to develop line speed. It can be assisted with hip rotation in both casting directions. The longer the stroke, the less severe the angle will be between the rod tip and the line. A long stroke makes it easier to

The Eastern casting style.

accelerate a cast for those who don't have great strength and speed. It is also good for casting heavy flies because it promotes smooth acceleration and deceleration when you stop the rod hand. On the downside, the farther back the rod hand goes, the greater the chance of the rod wandering out of the casting plane on long casts. This can collapse the loop upon delivery. The rod hand travels back and forth in a plane about 18 inches to the side of the caster's body. This path being so far from the caster's eyes makes precise aiming difficult.

The second is the "baseball" or Western casting style which is performed with the upper arm outward from the body as much as 90 degrees and the rod hand stopping at the height of the caster's head. The forearm should be approximately vertical, depending on casting trajectory. The upper arm should not be above horizontal or it can cause injury. On the backcast, the shoulder rotates enough

The Western casting style.

for the elbow to move on an upward arc. The rod hand usually stops at the height of the caster's ear and uses the most conservative stroke length possible as a default, which helps limit tracking errors. Casters who use this style often use "drift" (see p. 96) on the backcast to reposition the casting hand further back for long delivery casts. The elbow leads on this delivery. Joan Wulff uses and teaches this Western style, even though she was first taught in New Jersey.

The rod angle is almost upright as the default, unless conditions or obstructions require side arm. A nearly upright rod plane helps accuracy, since the leader has a tendency to "kick" beyond straight, as in the tuck cast. This occurs because of the momentum of a fast-unrolling loop that is stopped abruptly. If this occurs, it would still be in line with the target. In the case of a rod plane canted to one side, the leader has a tendency to kick to the other. Gravity will not assist in making a straight layout of a cast made in a horizontal plane. The amount of residual line speed transferred to the end of the line and leader will determine the layout. Too slow and it won't straighten, too fast and it will swing around past straight. Keeping the rod tip high during a cast also helps prevent the fly hitting the ground, water, or low obstructions. Grounding can ruin a hook point.

For short to medium casts, stopping the hand near the face helps your aim. It's like throwing darts. The rod hand moves in a downward arc during the stroke on short to medium casts. The arm and rod hand move less with this style than the Eastern style. For longer casts, the casting shoulder should be opened up to increase range of motion and the upper arm will be approximately 90 degrees to the cast on the backcast, before forward delivery. Tim Rajeff, elite

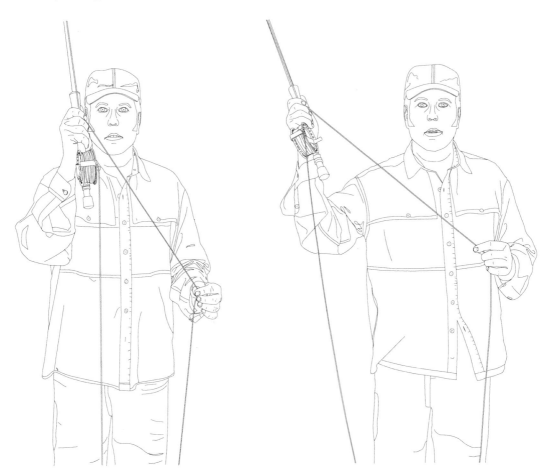

This is a variable casting style. Instead of using only one, it has a default style, then varies for different uses.

instructor, casting tournament veteran, and tackle manufacturer told me he stops his rod hand in front of his face for short casts and moves his rod plane outward and lengthens his stroke when increasing casting distance. Joan Wulff stops her rod hand on her hat brim for short casts and farther out and behind for long casts. She, too, has a variable stroke style. This variable stroke can be used with any rod grip.

TIMING AND TEMPO

Proper timing while overhead casting is waiting long enough for the loop to almost straighten before making the next cast. During the pause, the cast is straightening while gravity is acting on the line and fly in a downward direction. The amount of time you pause and let the cast straighten before beginning the next cast is critical to its success.

The duration of the pause between forward and backcasts can be too short, correct, or too long. Ideally, I like to start the next cast when the line is straight with no slack. Bruce Richards suggests ignoring the shape of the unrolling leader, since it has little mass compared to the line. There is an ongoing debate over the cues for starting a cast. Some say they can feel the straightening line make a tug, others use visual cues. I think the tug isn't from the line but the bounce of the rod tip after unloading. If you make a backward rod stroke without a line, you will still feel this

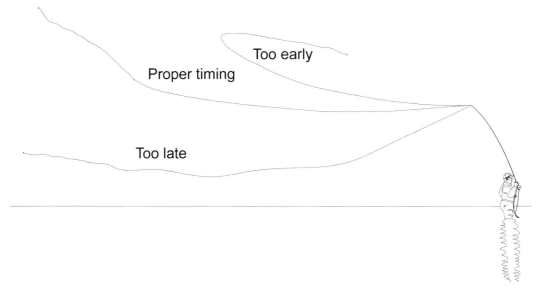

The object in proper backcast timing is to begin the forward cast when you can tension the whole extended line.

bounce because of the inertia of the rod. After the caster stops the rod, its mass flexes downward then it rebounds. If someone's reaction to this causes them to start the cast at the right time, great!

In Lefty Kreh's book, *Modern Fly Casting Method*, Lyons Press 2003, p. 137, Lefty suggests using a visual cue and teaches us to start a forward stroke, "... when you see that it is beginning to take on the appearance of a 'J', or a candy cane laid on its side, start sweeping your rod forward." He says, by the time the action is performed, with the slight delay of reaction time, the line of the backcast has straightened properly.

Another type of timing in overhead casting is tempo, or pace. This refers to the speed of the stroke. Assuming there is no wind, forward and back false casts should be made with the same tempo. It is best to use only as much line-speed as needed to make a cast with good tension and smoothness. A slow tempo is efficient for short casts, since the amount of line extended is short and there is less mass and the line is not in the air long enough for gravity to have much of an effect. This is also a necessary discipline for short-range presentations to spooky fish. A fast tempo is needed to keep long casts aloft because of the additional line weight and time in the air. Increasing tempo can help reduce line sag due to gravity and effects of wind drift as well. If you're casting with or against wind, you might have to mix the tempo by casting faster into the wind and slower with it. When you increase line speed, you will have to decrease the length of the pause correspondingly. The ability to adjust timing automatically is one sign of mastery.

Good timing while Spey casting is similar to that in overhead casting. Here, good timing is waiting long enough for the fly line or leader to adequately anchor, so it doesn't slip and lose the load for the forward cast. It is also waiting for a D to take shape but before it deforms and the underside contacts the water. A full D-loop will load the rod but excessive anchoring hampers the forward cast. Good timing also includes not waiting more than necessary before performing casts with sinking flies and lines that have long set-ups, like Skagit casts. The deeper they sink, the harder they are to lift into D-loop or cast.

TIMING FAULTS & CURES (OVERHEAD CASTS)

If you start your forward cast too early and the loop is still unrolling to the rear, the cast will force it open, causing a shock wave and even a crack, like a whip. That can occur because you use part of the forward energy and stroke just to open the loop before acting on the whole extended line. This will not make an efficient forward cast.

Rod preload is a myth that supposes that while the line is still moving during the pause, the force will bend the rod backward and store energy in it, or preload it for the next cast. By the time the line is almost straight on the backcast, it is hardly moving. The amount of rod-bend from this is inconsequential compared to the casting stroke's contribution to rod loading. The caster can intentionally add tension before making the forward cast, as I'll describe in the chapter on distance casting. A little tension in the line does prevent slack during the pause.

After you make the cast, gravity pulls down on the line and lowers your intended trajectory. It can fall beyond 180 degrees from your aiming point. If you wait too long, the loop will deform from gravity, lose tension, and become slack. If the trajectory is too low, the fly might "tick" on the backcast, which scares fish, causes slack, and if it hits a rock, it can ruin your hook. You can only load the rod with the portion of the line that is relatively straight or under tension. The cast is not acting upon the weight of the slack portion of the line. This portion will become the top leg of the forming loop and will likely not be parallel to the rod leg of the loop in flight. This lack of energy and deformity in the fly leg will make an inefficient cast with poor turnover.

Most of these faults are in the backcast and you should try to identify them by watching. If your backcast has adequate line speed but the line is falling too much, start the forward cast sooner. Ed Jaworawski wrote in his book *Troubleshooting the Cast*, Stackpole Books, 1999, p. 17, " . . . begin your forward motion when the last part of the line looks like a fish hook, candy cane, or a J. . . . " I know Ed's friend Lefty has mentioned the "J" on many occasions too. On the other hand, if you try this and you're cracking the whip by starting too early, watch the end of the line and start a little later, when it's almost straight.

LOOP FAULTS

Bill Gammill's foundational book, *The Essentials of Fly Casting* is one of the most enduring casting manuals. My understanding of his description is that rod tip can only make three paths in the vertical plane when performing a straight-line cast. If the acceleration is constant and rod arc and length is sufficient, the rod tip should have a straight-line path and result in a tight

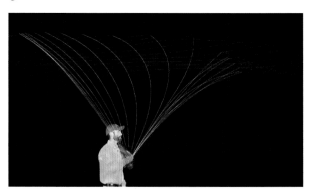

This stroboscopic photo of Kevney Moses making a forward false cast shows SLP, a straight line path of the rod-tip between loading and the beginning of the stop sequence. Also note what follows in counterflex and rebound to influence the loop. SLP and the characteristics of the stop are requirements for a tight loop.

This stroboscopic photo of a forward false cast shows a convex rod-tip path, which produces a wide loop, no matter how brief the stop.

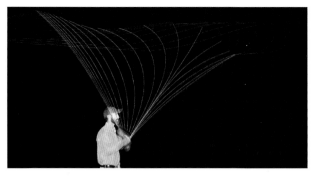

This stroboscopic photo of a forward false cast shows a concave rod-tip path caused by an abrupt acceleration at the beginning of a stroke of proper length. This cast produces a tailing loop.

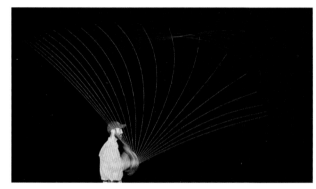

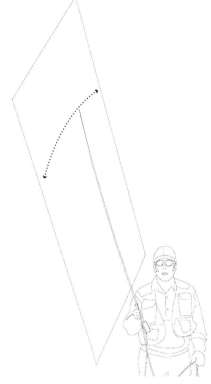

Adherence to one plane during a cast makes loops whose legs are in the same plane. This is important for accuracy and distance.

loop with parallel legs. A concave path produces a tailing loop. The last path is a convex shape, or the shape of an igloo. This rod tip path produces a large, open loop.

In the horizontal plane, the rod hand can either travel in a straight line or deviate from it, left or right. If the rod hand travels in a straight line without twisting or rotating in or out, the rod and rod tip will also travel in one plane. If the rod hand deviates, it causes the rod tip to deviate too.

TAILING LOOP FAULT

In 2003, I sent video I took of ACA tournament distance champions to FFF Board of Casting Governors Member, Macauley Lord, and also posted it on YouTube. The video helped us see what the loop does in flight. The fly leg of a loop on the most elite casters falls below the rod leg during long casts, due to gravity. It illustrated an acceptable loop we call a closed loop. Spey and roll casts use a closed loop. This helped us change the definition of a tailing loop, which used to include closed loops, and called it a fault.

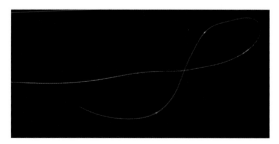

A tailing loop will prevent good turnover, accuracy, and distance. If the end goes through the loop, it will tighten and become a wind knot, whether it's breezy or not.

A tailing loop has a closed loop and an upward curve in the end of the fly leg and leader. In the most egregious tailing loop, the fly leg also crosses the rod leg of the loop twice and resembles a figure eight on its side as in the accompanying photo. A tailing loop is almost always caused by an abrupt acceleration somewhere in the stroke, causing a concave rod tip path. In other words, the rod tip dipped during the cast and the rod tip path resembled the inside of a bowl. The exception is when a cast violates the 180-degree angle rule with steep upward trajectories on both the back and forward casts. A stroke and haul in combination must be properly combined to load the rod and accelerate the line properly or faults such as tailing loops can occur. There are at least five ways a caster produces tailing loops.

The first and most common way, when everything else is right, is accelerating and loading the rod abruptly at the beginning of the stroke. To cure this, the caster should smoothly accelerate from the beginning to the end of the cast. Reducing line speed is also a good way to smooth out the stroke. Remember though, whenever you change line speed, always readjust the length of the pause.

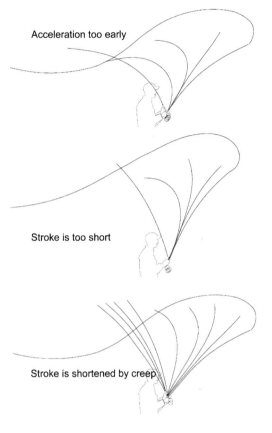

Top Three Causes of Tailing Loops

Acceleration too early

Stroke is too short

Stroke is shortened by creep

If a diagnosis isn't available, either try lengthening the stroke or increase the smoothness of the acceleration.

The second cause of a tailing loop is making a cast with insufficient rod arc. This occurs when the effective casting stroke is too short. The recommended cure is to add some translation, or an increase in the linear length of the casting stroke. The third cause is "creep." Creep is unintentional movement of the rod-hand in the direction of the cast, without loading the rod. This shortens effective stroke length. The rod hand must not move in the casting direction during the pause until the fly line straightens and the caster starts to load the rod. I tell students to have their rod-hand "freeze" during the pause and it usually works. If it doesn't, another cure for a tailing delivery cast is to incorporate drift after the backcast stop. Drift is an intentional rearward movement to increase potential forward stroke length or arc (see Chapter 6: Maximizing Casting Distance). The old corollary goes, if you're moving backward, you can't be creeping forwards.

Drag is a motion similar to creep. Drag differs because it is an intentional rod hand movement in the direction of the forward cast for the purpose of eliminating slack and repositioning the rod hand in preparation for a distant delivery cast (See distance chapter). When performed correctly, drag shouldn't cause a tailing loop. Dr. Gary Eaton, DO, IFFF MCI says, "It's OK to be a drag, but it's not OK to be a creep."

The fourth cause of a tailing loop is slowing the stroke prematurely. It will cause the rod to straighten prematurely and unload. When it straightens, the tip rises and forms a concave path. Using a rod that is too stiff for a given line can contribute to the same affect. Fifth is a cast that violates the 180-degree rule with steep upward trajectories on both the back and forward casts, like a steeple cast.

WIDE LOOP FAULT

I consider a wide loop to be a loop measuring greater than four feet between the fly leg and the rod leg. If a caster tries to cast a tight loop and the only result is a wide loop, there is a defect in the caster's mechanics or equipment. There are three ways to cast a wide loop when making a forward and backcast. The first is to cast with a convex rod tip path on both casts by using too much rod arc, as illustrated above. Even prolonging a stop can cause a wide loop without a caster realizing it. The most common cause is flexing the wrist too much. When someone first starts casting, they should not use their wrist to cast until they can cast a good loop and then learn to incorporate wrist rotation for more speed and distance. When someone adds wrist flexion, they must use the same rod arc as before. Otherwise, the arc and resulting loop will become larger. When you advance and need more line speed, adding wrist movement is imperative.

The second way a caster casts a wide loop is to use too much rod arc on one of the casts; either the backcast or forward cast. For example, a good forward cast is made but the caster drops the wrist on the backcast and makes a wide loop. If the 180-degree principle is followed, the loop shape should be correct, but if the backcast is directed too low and with too much force, the loop will form an "L" shape instead of a "J." The counterflex of the rod is directing the rod leg downward and the fly leg upward. I believe IFFF MCI Ed Jaworowski was the first one to document this. He did so in his book, *Troubleshooting the Cast* (Stackpole, 1999).

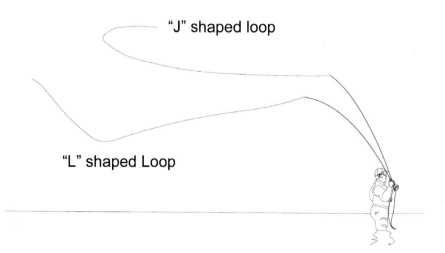

"J" shaped loop

"L" shaped Loop

A J-shaped loop is preferable because the L-shaped loop lacks good turnover to be effective, and a backcast with an L usually violates the 180-degree principle.

Faults in a backcast are easy to make, since they are behind our field of view. In the words of Norman Maclean in *A River Runs through It,* "Well, until man is redeemed he will always take a fly rod too far back . . . " I recommend properly watching the backcast when needed. To correct the cause of wide loops, note where you stop the rod at the ends of the stroke and use less rod arc as needed. You know you've shortened the stroke too much if you're accelerating smoothly, adhering to the 180-degree angle rule and suddenly you're casting a tailing loop. Another way to create too much arc in your cast is to accelerate a soft rod with "full speed" from beginning to end of the stroke, or stop to stop. The rod will bend and the tip will direct the line in a curve, instead of making a straight line.

Sometimes, making a backcast with excessive arc becomes a habit. If you have this one, try using these cures. One of Gordy Hill's cures for "wristing" is to squeeze the index and thumb on grip during the backcast stop of the rod. The muscle contraction this causes temporarily adds some stiffness to the wrist. Another cure taught to me by the late Captain Tom White of Marathon, FL, was the one he called, "Turn it Upside Down." By placing the reel against the inside of your forearm, you can't use your wrist. Macauley Lord calls this corrective aid, "Invert the Reel." He also taught me another trick many years ago. Wear a long sleeve shirt and tuck the rod butt into your cuff to hold it rigid until the new stroke is assimilated. If you still can't break the habit, The Royal Wulff Wristlok and the patent pending EaziCast™ wrist support and casting aid designed by Patrick Tennyson of Ireland are a few commercially available aids you can use to limit wrist mobility until the feeling of a proper stroke becomes automatic. These tools are a last resort, but can be effective.

ROD PLANE

During an overhead cast, the rod should theoretically travel in one plane from stop to stop. This is called the rod plane. The angle of this plane is measured relative to vertical, or 90 degrees from horizontal. If the rod deviates from this plane and does not track straight, the fly leg will wander out of parallel to the rod leg and cause problems. The more vertical the rod plane, the more vertical the resulting loop legs, but the rod shouldn't be perfectly vertical or the fly and leader can strike the rod. Therefore, canting the rod tip slightly outward from vertical is the best compromise. If you cast in a near horizontal rod plane, the loop will also follow the same angle because of centrifugal force and gravity.

ROD PLANE (TRACKING) FAULTS

This concept goes back to what Bill Gammel taught us about a straight rod tip path. If during a cast, the rod butt were to theoretically cut through a horizontal sheet of glass like a glass cutter and we could see the cut, the path should be straight across. If the rod hand and subsequently the rod wavered in some way, it will cause a deviation in the rod-tip path. This would be a tracking error. As a result, the loop will twist and the fly leg will not be parallel with the rod leg. This hurts the aerodynamics of the cast and this loop will probably fail to turn over and straighten. This can rob massive amounts of distance and accuracy, not to mention a tangled landing.

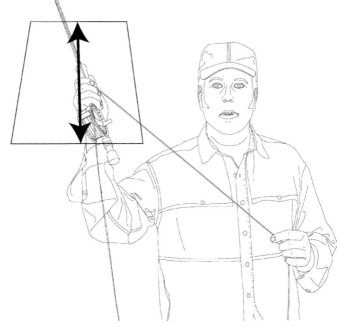

When you extend and retract your arm, using the shoulder, elbow, and wrist joints, they must make the correct compound movements or the path of the rod hand won't be straight. The farther you bring your casting hand rearward, the harder it will be to track straight. If your hand isn't tracking straight, the rod won't be either. One of the biggest causes of poor tracking is excessive forearm rotation on

This visual analogy helps envision the path of the hand for good tracking.

the backcast. Since the rod handle and rod blank are not exactly inline with or parallel to the forearm when you cast, any forearm twisting will cause an eccentric movement of the rod-tip. Although it's good to relax the grip after the stop, many casters let the wrist droop to the side during the stop. This is one place the fault occurs. If you have muscle memory of throwing a football or baseball, it might cause curving motions in your casting stroke. For example, we're taught to set up to throw a football with an inward wrist rotation to cock the wrist almost behind the ear and then cross the body on the follow-through after the release.

To find out where your tracking is, you can take video of your cast with the camera in front of or behind the rod, showing the tip. Cast at or above the camera. Casting in front of a golf mirror or reflective window can also show your tracking. Joan Wulff often reminds us to always use targets for both backcast and forward casts to maintain their 180-degree relation to each other.

I think casting down an outstretched rope or set of targets is the best exercise to cure tracking errors and is a good maintenance drill. The stripes of an athletic field sideline work well but you can't move them relative to the wind. You should either cast downwind or with the wind on your non-casting side.

My preference is to arrange four small fluorescent plastic sport cones at 25-foot intervals in a straight line 100 feet long. Place a fifth cone in the middle of the line and stand back so your rod tip is directly over the middle cone when it is held in your normal casting plane. If you don't keep your tip traveling over the line, you will be casting in a long triangle. Now false cast using the cones as targets in front and back. The true test is not to look at the backcast, just let the backcast land without making a forward cast. Now turn and look where it landed, taking any side-wind drift into consideration. If the line lands in line with the cones, super. If not, make a backcast aiming down the line, making sure your body isn't twisted and look at the alignment of your arm to the target and the angles you need to make the cast. Make a few false casts and retest the backcast until it's tracking true. If you are aware of where your backcast is going and how your loop is unrolling, you can set up for great forward casts.

Tim Rajeff was first to show me this trick for checking my stroke. He instructed me to extend the index finger of my casting hand to represent the rod and had me lightly drag it across the side of building while making a stroke with it. The object was not to lose contact, thus maintaining straightness. A plate glass window is easier on the nails! You can also watch the amount of joint movement and angles used to maintain straightness and recall them when casting a rod and reel.

If you're serious about good fundamentals for distance, this drill can help cure tracking errors and reinforce good form.

TRAJECTORY

The trajectory of a cast is the angle between the water level and the initial direction of the loop in flight. If a cast is made toward a specific target, this relationship and angle should compensate for elevation difference between the caster and the target. If the caster is on a boat or jetty, the angle will be greater to a given target than if wading. We establish this angle to avoid objects, mainly on a backcast and to reach our intended target, whether they are at twenty feet or 100.

The trajectory of a cast should also be based on the desired casting distance and the anticipated effect of gravity, wind carry, or wind resistance. Ideally, the energy of a cast should transfer down the line and open the loop and leader just before the fly reaches the target. Gravity will also have a greater negative affect on casts in an upward angle compared to those made "down hill." We almost always aim our casts 180 degrees apart in order to direct the energy of the next cast toward our next target. For example, a low forward cast requires a high backcast. All other variables being equal, due to gravity, casting trajectory should also vary with line density and the weight and resistance of the fly.

It pays to use a higher backcast when casting a heavy fly or high-density line. Even when using the proper pause timing on a cast, these heavier-than-normal payloads will fall faster than a floating line of the same weight with a light fly. Which falls faster, a ton of feathers or a ton of lead? A caster can use trajectory in her favor in windy conditions. This will be covered in greater detail in Chapter 6.

LINE CONTROL AND SLACK

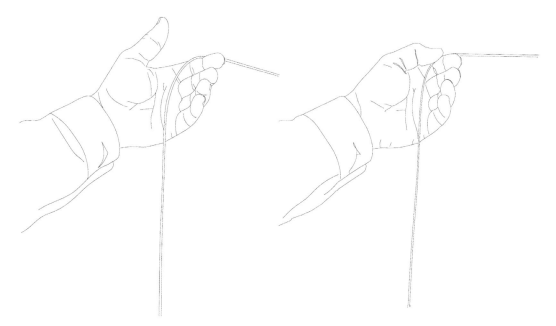

These drawings show line running over the palm while shooting line and the stop to drop the fly where you want it. This basic technique helps get the fly to moving fish quickly.

Slack should be eliminated unless it is intentionally included in a cast for presentation purposes. Ally Gowens, IFFF MCI from Britain, uses the phrase, "organize the line," to mean taking up slack before making a pick-up. Slack prevents the efficient transfer of energy from rod to line. Try to eliminate slack whenever trying to load a rod or set a hook. The simplest way is to keep the rod tip as low as possible and always strip-in slack. Holding or stacking loops will help you organize line. To control line when lengthening a cast by slipping line, use your index finger to pinch the line to the handle when false casting and strip line off the reel with the line hand. Pinch the line between the index, middle, and thumb on your line hand. You alternately let the line run over your palm, then stop it by pinching. You can always shoot, mend or wiggle line out when needed. I'll cover shooting and hauling later.

ROLL CASTS

The roll cast is so important and fundamental; it is arguably the first cast a new fly angler should learn. The main use of a roll cast is to replace an overhead cast when you don't have enough room to make a proper backcast. You can make a roll cast to straighten out and eliminate the slack of minor line messes beyond the rod tip. A roll cast is most readily made with a floating line, since the line is left on the water until you make the cast. A sinking line makes lifting the line to the surface for pick-up more difficult. You can bring heavy lines and flies to the surface making one or more roll casts in order to make a water-loaded or aerial backcast. Making them in combination will also add distance. A roll cast pick-up is a roll cast directed above the water so you can perform an aerial backcast as soon as the line straightens. It can also be used to quickly and quietly lift a popper off the water, or as John Alden Knight used it fifty years ago, as a set-up for a change-of-direction cast.

Good roll casts require the D-loop, anchor, fly, and target to be aligned. This is an extension of the 180-degree principle.

This is the off-shoulder roll cast used to help align the cast to prevent a crossed loop, or to keep the D-loop downwind when excessive wind is on the casting side.

The roll cast is a "dead-line" water-anchored cast using a hanging D-loop and water tension to load the rod. In other words, you drag the loop into position and pause before making the forward stroke. In its simplest form, the roll cast is a straight-line cast without a change of direction. As with all water anchored casts, the 180-degree principle applies; the D-loop, leader, and fly must be in a line 180 degrees opposite the target. This directs the cast efficiently, quietly, and safely toward your target. When making a roll cast, you can aim the D-loop opposite your target by sliding it into alignment alongside your body on your casting side. If your fly line, leader, and fly are in front of you and you try to cast, it will cause a crossed loop and will probably tangle. If your fly line, leader, and fly cannot be slid into good alignment, change the side of your body you make the cast by tilting the rod tip over the opposite side as in the off-shoulder cast. You can get extra angle by reaching your casting hand backward over your head. To make a tight loop, accelerate the casting rotation of the arm and wrist to the highest speed at the end of the stroke. This will keep the rod tip moving in a relatively straight line.

If you need to make a very short roll cast but it doesn't seem you have enough line to achieve an anchor, try kneeling or squatting, so more line will lie on the water. On the other hand, if you need to make a long cast, there are four techniques you can use in conjunction with a tight loop. The first is to move as much of the D-loop behind you as possible. You do this by slowly lifting almost all the line off the water and jump it to the anchor point so the line leader connection is about a rod's length away and pause. Throwing the D-loop backward is only possible if you have enough room behind you. Lift as much of the line off the water as possible by raising your rod tip and make the forward cast.

The second technique is to use a side-arm stroke and bring the rod tip back and away from the casting shoulder. This set-up also maximizes the length of line in the D-loop with which to load the rod and increases stroke length potential. Before making the cast, lift the D-loop off the water with the rod tip to reduce the length of line adhering to the water from water tension and causing resistance to your lift. Then, accelerate into the cast and end with a positive stop. Third, is to use weight transfer back and forth to create momentum for the cast. Joan Wulff is adamant about this. Lastly, you can also increase line speed and thus distance by adding a haul in the forward delivery. Remember to observe the 180-degree principle with your rod tip, D-loop, and fly.

The Z-Mend is a quick way to increase the length of line for a roll cast, commonly used in the roll cast round of the ACA Trout Fly Accuracy event. Strip out the measured amount of line needed to make the cast. Elevate the reel until the rod tip is almost in the water and wiggle the rod tip from side to side to stack-mend line in the water. You regulate the slipping line with the line hand and the water tension anchors the line so each rod movement lays out more line. Then bring the rod tip back as far as needed to make and direct the D-loop opposite the target. Then make the cast. You can also submerge the tip and snap gently up to pull more line out of the rod tip.

ROLL CAST FAULTS

When performing roll casts, a few things can occur to prevent you from achieving safe, accurate, and long casts. The first is "hooking," which is when the caster makes a good D-loop side-arm, then moves the rod tip in a vertical plane to set for the forward cast. The D-loop then has

When a caster hooks the D-loop behind with the rod tip, it's a called a roll cast hook fault. The cast set-up is poorly aligned.

to be pulled sideways to be cast in the direction the rod is moving. If that happens to you, just concentrate on keeping the rod tip over the D-loop when making the cast.

The next problem in a roll cast is the inability to cast a tight loop. Assuming the set-up and alignment are correct, the problem is in the rate of acceleration. If the rod is accelerated too early in the stroke, it will cause a convex rod-tip path. This domed path causes wide loops just like it does in an overhead cast. To fix the problem, accelerate the rod smoothly from beginning to end. The wrist should add rotation at the end of the stroke and for long roll cast, transferring your weight from back to the front will help line speed. Chuck Easterling, IFFF MCI, has a saying to help cure large roll cast loops using the clock metaphor. He says: "No power till midnight!"

Chris Korich put together a lesson called The Flicking Drill that contains three reference points with key words for his roll cast at a 40-foot target. He advocates the use of a firm wrist. The first is the Top Position—vertical arm. Second, relax your shoulder, let gravity pull the arm and rotate down till the rod is vertical at the Middle Position. Third, flick down until the forearm is level at the Bottom Position. As simple as this is, it can help teach the roll cast and correct several faults.

PICK-UPS

This spiral pick-up is so fun to perform, it can become overused.

When you pick up a floating line from the water, you must first overcome water tension. The quietest way to do this and best way to eliminate slack, is to start with the rod tip at water level and slowly lift the rod tip and accelerate into your backcast. If you rip it out fast, it will make excessive noise and prematurely load the rod. Using a haul will assist lifting a long length of fly line on a pick-up. Delay the haul until the rod is at about a 45-degree angle above the water since that is when the acceleration of the stroke begins. Otherwise, the haul will create slack. There are a few pick-ups that excel for particular uses.

The spiral pick-up is like a snake roll, but instead of making a change of direction, you just continue the lift into the backcast. As a righty, I perform it counterclockwise. It's a good choice when picking up a weighed fly because it planes the line to the surface with little commotion. The spiral pick-up is also useful in quietly picking-up a dry fly because it lifts, instead of slides the line.

Another good pick-up maneuver is the roll cast pick-up. When you fish a popper and try to lift it and the line out of the water with the rod, it'll throw water and make gurgling sounds. That's not good if you're trying not to scare fish. Instead, throw a roll cast aimed above the fly. The resulting loop should turn the leader over and pluck the fly out of the water backwards with little splash or noise. When the leader straightens with the fly out of the water, accelerate into your backcast to present the popper again. This cast can also be used with a dry fly if there is a lot of current and you don't want to drown your fly.

There are several options for picking up a sinking line or a heavy fly, or both. If there is a possibility of a strike while stripping a fly all the way in on a heavy line, then by all means strip it all the way. With little line outside the guides, you can start by making very slow tip-casts and shoot line in both directions. As the length increases you can also accelerate. You can lay the fly in the water and also roll cast and shoot in either direction. If you only expect a strike in the first few feet of your retrieve with a heavy line, you can roll cast one or more times until the fly comes to the surface, or use a roll cast pick-up, if the fly isn't too heavy.

LENGTHENING AND SHORTENING LINE (WITHOUT HAULING)

Adjustments in cast length require good line handling to maintain control and prevent tangles. Shooting or slipping line can be performed either on the backcast, forward cast, or both. Shooting is when you release/let line from the line hand close to the rod stop and let the cast pull line through the guides. Slipping line is when you release the line and let it slip through your line hand, then seize it again in your fingers and make a false, or presentation cast. I don't recommend adding line into strong wind unless you can do it with a tight loop and without introducing slack. Otherwise the cast might not turn over.

When aiming a cast at a given target, you have to get the cast length correct, as well as left and right accuracy. The way to do this with the most control is to false cast with the line pinned against the handle with the index finger of the casting hand. You can shorten the cast by stripping line back through the index finger with the line hand. To extend the cast, you can loosen the index finger and let small amounts slip through, until the length is right. Or, you can release the line from that index finger and make adjustments with the line hand. I like to slip and adjust length with the line hand.

When trying to extend a cast as far as possible without hauling, you can let the line shoot through your fingers or release the line completely from the line hand. If you need to stop it at an exact spot, letting it run through your fingers lets you stop it precisely. If you're blind casting or distance casting, letting go is better, since it reduces friction.

HAULING

A haul is a properly timed tug on the line below the stripper guide for the main purpose of adding acceleration to the cast. In addition, it can be used to increase tension on the fly line and eliminate slack, which helps the stroke load the rod. A haul does load the rod a little, but in comparison to the load provided by the rod hand, it's not significant. Hauling increases casting distance and helps combat wind. When casting in windy conditions, you've got to use high line speed to defeat it, but, once again, don't shoot too much line into the wind. It's more effective to shoot more line downwind on the presentation. Hauling the line in conjunction with good rod speed will accelerate the line faster than the rod hand alone.

When hauling or holding line in the line hand, you pinch the line between the thumb, index, and, optionally, the middle finger. The fewer fingers involved, the easier it will be to release the line cleanly. You can haul, shoot, and recapture the line in the line hand repetitively in a shooting, hauling sequence.

The haul mirrors the stroke. This matter of timing means when the rod hand is accelerating the rod, the hauling hand should be accelerating the line.

Generally, hauls should mirror the timing of the rod hand. The acceleration of a fly line should be constant. Since a haul does contribute slightly to rod loading, which bends the rod, having the fastest part of the tug near the end of the stroke helps the rod tip travel in straight line. The length of the haul should correspond to the length of the cast being made: the longer the cast, the longer the haul, the shorter the cast, the shorter the haul should be. This will help prevent slack if the haul is too long. The hauling speed should also be relative to the speed used in the rod stroke.

A haul is just a tug and can be combined with shooting line by releasing at the same time as the rod stop. You add a haul by pulling down on the line below the stripper guide during a false cast to add some line speed or to shoot or slip line to lengthen or deliver a cast. You might use a haul when delivering a roll cast. It's also used in tournament distance casting to complete the turnover (see Chapter 5).

A single-haul is a single pull and return used on either a forward cast or backcast. You might false cast using a single-haul only into the wind or for a pick-up. The double-haul is a continuous cycle of hauls with accommodation for returning a length of line into the cast equal to the length of the haul. If you hauled down during a false cast, you would end with your line hand extended, unable to repeat the haul. It is used for shooting line, combatting wind, and generating the greatest line speed for the longest one-handed casts.

You start a double-haul with a tug on the line at the beginning of the stroke and without letting go of the line at the stop, return line up through the guides during the pause. In the double-haul, there are two parts. The haul on the forward cast is a downward pull and the return on the backcast is an upward motion of the line hand. The length of these movements should be of equal lengths when making casts of equal distance without any headwind. Uneven hauls nullify line speed and casting potential. Under these conditions, the rod movement and double hauling should be symmetrical on both casts. Hauls for defeating wind are addressed in Chapter 6.

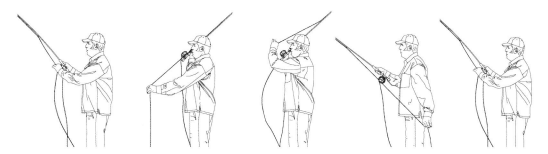

This sequence of the double haul starts with a backcast and ends with a forward cast, without releasing or shooting line. Those are optional.

The first motion is down, the second is up. Steve Rajeff likes to teach the haul by saying, "bounce" when the line hand stops and the haul changes directions. Learning the double haul by pantomiming eliminates the distraction of tackle, as first taught publicly in the US by Mel Krieger. We often describe the movement of the hands doing a double haul as: hands apart, hands together, or the line hand goes down, and up. To prevent slack, the rate you return the hauled line should match the line's pull upward though the guides. The angle at which you haul should be down, beginning forward and slightly away from the reel, or line can wrap on both the reel and rod butt. If you make a haul at too great an angle outward, it can cause line resistance and even pull the rod in that direction and out of plane.

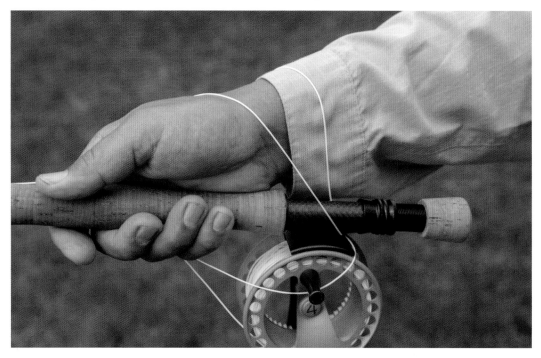

This mess is most often the result of inadequate hauling angle.

Double hauling makes it possible to carry longer lengths of line in the air than without it. Hauling helps eliminate slack in the cast. It also adds a little load to the rod. You can use it when false casting, lengthening line, or for the delivery. On the delivery, you have the option of holding onto the line if you have enough line stripped out to reach your target, or you can release the line from your line hand and shoot more. In tournament distance casting, some casters watch the loop unroll before it lands and yank the line to guarantee compete leader turnover to gain a few extra feet. That's called a check-haul or triple-haul.

When casting at your limits of distance and good form with the rod hand alone, adding hauling will not only increase this distance, but will distribute some of the work to the line hand and lighten the effort in your stroke. This can reduce arm fatigue when casting for long periods. It also has another effect: hauling helps you achieve greater line speed without loading or bending the rod as much. This should keep a straighter tip path and the resulting loops should be tighter. Paul Arden's interpretation of Lowell-Grunde's motion capture study supports these assumptions.

Double hauls for forward and backcasts don't have to be symmetrical, just as strokes don't have to be either. If one casting direction is into the wind, your stroke and haul should be faster in that direction and slower downwind. If you accelerate the line normally, plus gain assistance from the wind, excessive line speed can cause unwanted rod shock and counterflex during rod deceleration.

According to *Field & Stream* editor A. J. McClane in a May 1975 article, "Historically, the double haul was first used by Stanley Forbes in a tournament at the 1915 World's Fair in San Francisco." He also explained that it didn't become popular among anglers until the early 1930s, when their tackle could be made reliable enough to use hauling without breakage.

HAULING FAULTS & CURES

Even with a good stroke, improper haul timing and acceleration can help cause a tailing loop or slack and the resulting wide loop. As with everything, an event is either correctly timed, timed too early, or timed too late. If your loop is too wide when you make a pick-up and the backcast is weak, the haul timing is probably too early. There is probably slack in the pick-up and the rod is not loading properly. If this is occurring, wait until your lift is accelerating into the last half of the backcast before hauling. The problem with hauling too late will be abruptness and a loss of potential acceleration. The haul shouldn't pull the tip down at the end of the cast or it will pull on the rod leg and open the loop. The haul should end as the rod decelerates and straightens. In casting geek terms, just before RSP.

If the acceleration and length of the haul is not relative to the stroke, it will cause incorrect loading or possibly slack. For example, if you haul abruptly at the beginning of the stroke, it can help cause a tailing loop by contributing to concavity in the rod-tip path.

One fault I see often is slack between the line hand and stripper guide on the return move. This is caused by a weak or unnecessarily long haul on the preceding cast for the amount of rod speed. Another similar fault is when a caster tries to return line faster than the cast is unrolling and the line above the hand loses tension. You can't push slack through the guides. Just slow down the return, or up-stroke, of the double-haul. You need sufficient line speed to pull line back into the guides. The length of the haul should be relative to the length of the cast. A short haul for a short cast and a long haul for a long cast. A short cast might need a 6-inch haul and long one might need a 3-footer.

One of the most common hauling faults I see is on the backcast. The caster holds the line in the line hand and makes the backcast but doesn't haul down with the line hand. To the caster, it looks like a proper haul is occurring because the hands are separating but the line is sliding through the guides without enough speed. To learn how to avoid this, move the line hand (with the line) in unison with the casting hand when false casting without hauling. When you do haul, your line hand will be trained to stay in the proper relationship, ready to make a haul.

Another problem when hauling is tangling line on the rod butt. Hauling or releasing line under the rod butt is the cause. As line coils tighten, one can lasso the rod butt. Also, when you make the return in a double-haul with your line hand below the reel, line can wrap. When you release the line to shoot it, slack will be pulled through the stripper guide, but if anything interrupts the flow of line through the guides, the line reaches out like an octopus and wraps the rod butt. If these things occur to you, guide the line to the side away from the rod or haul in a line where your line hand would pass the outside of your thigh.

The remedy for these problems is to learn to use proper mechanics, timing, and smooth acceleration. If you see errors while false casting and hauling, try without hauling to determine the cause: the stroke or the haul. Then you can make changes to the part causing the error.

RELEASE TIMING

Whether you're making a delivery cast with a haul or without, the moment of line release will have an effect on the cast. This also applies to roll and Spey casts. If the line is released too early, rod unloading will occur prematurely and energy will be lost. If the release is too late, you will feel the rod bend forward into counterflex and two things will happen. First, the rod tip will pull down on the line and waste forward energy. Secondly, this bending down of the rod-tip will pull the loop open. The best time to release the line into the cast is when the rod first straightens and the loop is formed. At this point, all the rod's available energy has been transferred to the line and the cast is on the way.

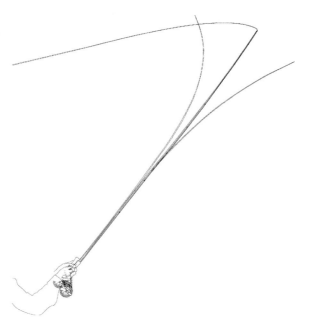

The best time to release your hold on the line for a delivery is when you sense the rod stop and not a millisecond after. The closer you release to RSP-1, the less the rod tip will open the cast.

CONTINUOUS TENSION AND OVAL CASTS

These casts are used when you have limited height or backcast room or when you have an adverse wind. They also help prevent the fly from striking the angler when using unbalanced rigs. These casts should be made with constant tension and without stopping the rod and letting the casts straighten, until the delivery.

The Belgian cast is performed by picking up the fly and swinging the rod tip sidearm in an oval path into the backcast and up to a near vertical position with constant tension that ends with a stop in the direction of the

This is the historic Belgian cast and has many practical uses. A U-shaped rod-hand stroke and constant movement set it apart.

intended target. The backcast never stops, so it does not straighten out. You do not have to present the fly on the forward cast and can false cast or add other combinations before presenting the fly. Hans Gebetsroither, guide and river keeper on Austria's River Traun, is credited as the originator of this cast we've called the Belgian cast since 1958. A Belgian tournament caster who was trained by Hans for the first international (official) casting championships (CIPS) in Brussels in 1958 used the oval cast Hans taught him and it was named the Belgian cast, not the Austrian cast, by spectators. Those who learned from Hans say he had many other oval and constant tension casts in his bag of tricks.

You make a continuous tension cast in one casting plane by making an elliptical stroke without a stop, until the delivery. The resulting rod-tip path is an oval but in one plane. Since the backcast doesn't straighten, it is useful when fishing where space is limited and under certain wind situations (see "Taming the Wind" in Chapter 4 and "TLT Academy" in Chapter 8).

ONE-HAND SPEY CASTS

When you don't have enough room for a backcast, you can use a roll cast. If you also need to change directions, as when swinging a fly in a stream or river, the best cast to do this is one of the Spey casts. Roll casts and Speys have water anchors using a D-loop in which the loop forms under the rod tip. You can perform all Spey casts with a single or double hand rod. Like the roll cast, they are waterborne, or water anchored, but they are active line roll casts with a change of direction. Spey casts are generally made from 45–90 degrees across the current to present a long swing or drift. You might even cast further upstream when you desire a line or fly to sink more deeply.

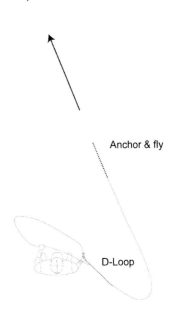

The anchor in a Spey cast is the end of the fly line, leader, and fly placed onto the water, in addition to the resistance of the D-loop, with which to load the rod.

The position for the anchor, regardless of the rod you're using, is on the same side the cast will be made; approximately one rod-length away and one rod's length away. You always place the anchor downwind. I like to change to my non-dominant hand when necessary and use my downwind hand to cast with instead of casting off-shoulder. There is also a universal reference for a caster's position in relation to the river flow. If you're facing across river and the flow is moving from left to right, you're on the "right bank." If you're looking at the flow moving right to left, you're on the "left bank." These positions are interchangeable with "river right" and "river left."

When the river has your fly awash downstream at the end of a drift, it is said to be "on the dangle." The resulting difference between a D- and a V-loop is line speed and distance. A V-loop will travel faster and cast farther than a D-loop and is more aerodynamic. Its shape also concentrates the energy in a forward direction more efficiently. You use a flatter stroke to make a V-loop and stop the rod. It's almost like a backcast. To form the D-loop, you use a more upward curving angle in the formation stroke and continue into the forward cast without a stop. As in the roll cast, you also need to observe the 180-degree principle, so you must align the fly, leader, and D-loop with the target.

Ideally, all casts should come off the water with a minimum of commotion that could scare fish. If the underside of the loop lies in the water, the

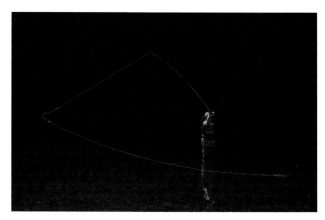

The D or V-loop in a Spey cast is like the backcast of an overhead cast. A V-loop is fastest and tightest and will load the forward cast better than a D-loop.

cast will be noisy and inefficient. This can be prevented by starting with the rod tip low, then directing the D- or V-loop upward. These loops function similarly to the backcast loops of an overhead cast. As the Spey master Way Yin says, "You make the loop under the rod tip." There are two groups of casts differentiated by the duration of the anchor before making the cast.

The first group is "kiss and go" casts, which includes traditional Spey and Scandinavian styles. You should make the cast as soon as the leader and the first few feet of line have landed. The other group is Skagit-style casts, which use a sustained anchor for setting up the line. You don't rush the cast and use the slightly deeper anchor to load the rod to move the heavy lines and flies you'd use for winter salmon or steelhead fishing. The Double-Spey and Snap-T and a few I won't cover here, are Skagit casts. Snaps are a new addition to Skagit casting. A caster forms a loop by accelerating the rod, then snapping back in the opposite direction. It is used in a Spey cast to position the line. Instead of lifting the line upstream as in a Double-Spey, you would snap it in place. This cast is called the Snap-T (see p. 47).

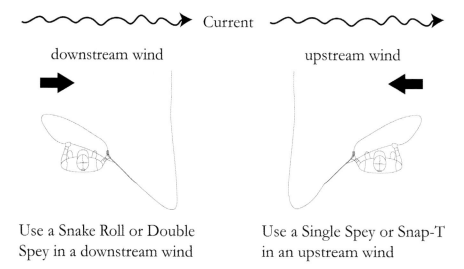

Wind direction dictates anchor placement and everything else follows. Flying hooks and line should be avoided.

The most important similarity among all Spey casts is the way they deal with wind from a safety standpoint. You always want to make your cast off your downwind side to avoid being hit by the line and/or fly. The way to do that is to place the anchor on the downwind side. Choose which cast to use with this in mind.

SWITCH CAST

The switch cast is an active line roll cast without a change of direction. The main use for it is teaching and practicing anchor placement, timing, and proper stroke. An open-water fisher could also use this cast when casting out and stripping flies to a shore or boat. It is the foundation upon which Spey casts revolve. It is a kiss-and-go cast. The easiest place to practice this cast is on still water. To make the cast, you

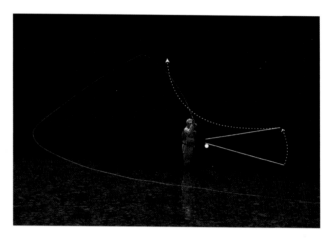

The set-up for the switch cast is a lift and sweep into the loop formation. The last step, not shown, is a forward cast with smooth acceleration.

lift the rod to about 20 degrees to break the water tension on the line and fly, and swing them to form the anchor about a rod's length away as you form the D-loop with an oval backcast into the key, or set position. In the key position, everything is aligned to the target and your rod, body, and D-loop are ready for launch. You can now make the forward cast with the rod tilted off-vertical.

THE SINGLE-SPEY

The single-Spey is the basic change-of-direction cast for moving water. This cast is made when you're fishing an upstream wind and the anchor is placed and the cast is made on the downwind side to keep the line and fly away from you. It's almost the same as the switch, with a rotation. When you need to make a change-of-direction cast from the dangle to across stream, you will need to reposition the line by lifting

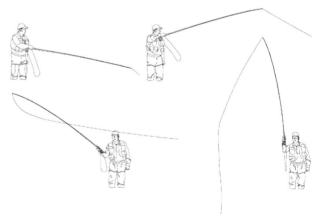

This drawing shows the steps of a single-Spey from the fly downstream on the dangle river left: the lift, sweep into D-loop formation and anchor placement, and immediate forward cast.

and starting a level sweep toward your anchor point, then blending into a rotational movement to form an upstream anchor 180 degrees away from your target. You make your D- or V-loop and move into your key position and make the cast.

THE SNAKE ROLL

The snake roll was not invented on the Snake River. Simon Gawesworth of England invented it and its aerial spiral resembles the uncoiling of a snake. If you form a funnel with your cast, it will bite you like a snake. This cast should be used when the wind is blowing downstream, and the anchor is placed downstream of you, to keep away from the teeth of the snake. It's a very quick and efficient cast. When you make this cast from the left bank, the rod rotation is clockwise and when you're on the right back, the rod rotation should be counter-clockwise. I remember this because I wear my "clock" on my left wrist. When I teach the snake roll to someone who is very coordinated, I ask him to mime jumping rope. The rotation for casting a snake roll with either hand is like the rotation of the hands when swinging a jump rope in the forward direction, or back to front.

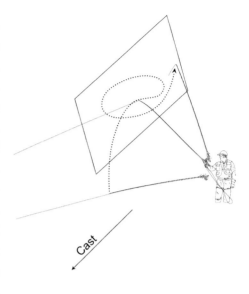

The snake roll requires a slow to fast acceleration while keeping the rod tip spiraling in one plane.

The snake roll begins with a continuous movement of the rod hand to lift almost all the line off the water and continuing into a slow horizontal slide of the rod toward the bank, leading into an oval spiral of the rod tip toward center river. Keep your rod tip in contact with an imaginary vertical plane, Simon calls it the blackboard, or the loop will spiral toward you uncontrollably. With slightly increasing speed, sweep the rod back and upward into the formation of a D-loop and anchor. Align the D-loop, anchor, and fly with the target and as soon as the line lands, you are ready to make the forward cast. To go back and explain a little, the initial slide toward the bank is to create tension and reposition the rod hand for the shape of the spiral stroke. The shape of the stroke determines the size and shape of the resulting D-loop. An oval stroke makes a lower, more efficient D-loop that will extend behind the caster. A round stroke will make a large D-loop that does not extend as much behind. There is a trade-off in Spey casting between efficient loop shapes and practicality. If you don't have room behind you, you must keep your loops round.

DOUBLE-SPEY

In instances when the wind is blowing downstream and you can't safely use the single-Spey, you are best using the double-Spey. The essential rod move is to lift and sweep the line from the dangle and form a loop of line all the way to your upstream side, stopping when the end of your line is almost opposite your target. You should adjust for current drift in this estimation since this point will be used to form your anchor. The ending point of your rod tip is upstream of you and near the water. Now, make an accelerating rising sweep with the rod tip into the key position, so the line pirouettes on the leader on your casting side as you form a D-loop and align the D, leader, fly, and target. When the leader is straight, you're ready to fire!

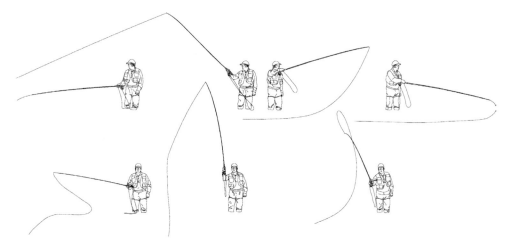

This double-Spey sequence begins with line on the dangle river right. Lift the line, sweep upstream to reposition the line about a rod's length out and lower the rod tip almost to the water when the line's end is located where you want the anchor. Change rod direction downstream and sweep with a low incline until the rod tip is over the end of the line and then upward to pirouette the leader into alignment and form the D-loop. Then immediately make the forward cast.

SNAP-T

If you're in a hurry and don't want to perform the double-Spey which requires lifting the line upstream, you can snap it! This is also a cast for an upstream wind. The snap starts like a fast sweep that ends in a reverse chopping stroke. You must calculate where you want the end of the line, which will be your anchor location on your downwind side. This snap will make the end of the line sail in the direction of the lift but leaving about half the line on the water in front of you. You can now lift that loop up and around to your key position and cast it out.

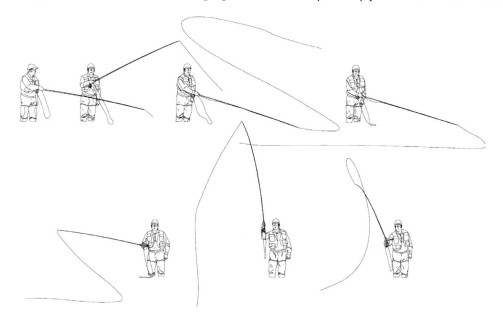

This Snap-T begins on river left with the line and fly awash and the first move is a lift and an upstream sweep upward until the rod is pointing 45 degrees downstream with the tip quite high. Then make a reverse snap sending the line upstream, out about a rod's length. Then a low angle sweep to lift the line from the water, align the leader and form the D-loop. Then immediately make the forward cast.

I've used Spey-casting techniques with ten-foot one-hand rods for Lake Ontario tributary steelhead since the 1990s. They're good for keeping line off the water, mending, and for making one-hand Spey casts. I remember one day on Oak Orchard Creek when I walked down from the hydro-dam and found an angler casting to a nice steelhead holding in a steeply cut side channel. He could not reach the right drift lane because of the lack of backcast room against the bank. So I waited out of sight for about ten minutes until he gave up. The wind was blowing hard downstream toward the lake, so I used a double-Spey with my one-hander and caught the twelve pound hen on the second cast.

SPEY FAULTS

All waterborne casts are subject to most of the same three major types of casting faults involving the anchor, regardless of whether using a one- or two-hand rod. The first fault involves bad anchor placement. The D-loop should be downwind on the casting side, about a rod's length away from the caster. If the anchor is too little or behind the caster, the anchor will have insufficient stick, or amount of water contact and the anchor will pull out and prevent sufficient rod load.

Let's assume these are river left single Spey anchor fault examples. If the anchor is too far upstream of a caster, the anchor will be misaligned with the D-loop and the target. This is called a Bloody L and the result is an inefficient load and the ripping of the anchor to free it. If the anchor is too far downstream, or somewhere in front of the caster, the attempted cast will cause a crossed loop. Instead of failing to free the line on the downstream dangle with a lifting move and sweeping it to where you want it, one might use too much speed and overshoot the intended anchor. To try and prevent this, make sure you lift just high enough to free the line from the water and then continue through the sweep motion with only enough speed to gently place the anchor. Try doing this mainly with body rotation. It the line isn't freed on the lift, it will load the rod so much it will be hard to control when it does break free.

The last common problem is too much line in the water, causing excessive stick. This is usually caused by three mistakes. The first is directing the D-loop back parallel to the water, or downward. In can also be caused by actually lowering the rod tip and losing tension in the bottom of the D-loop. This fault is called "Trunk." To prevent having the bottom of the D-loop in the drink, incorporate a small upward sweep of the rod tip at the end of the sweep before hitting the "key" position and drift the rod tip up a little, instead of rotating it back and down. Lastly, don't wait too long or excessive stick will be created. When you hit the key, it's time to cast.

CHAPTER 4

PRESENTATION CASTS

There is nothing quite as rewarding as when a properly-selected and executed cast results in the desired reaction from a fish: a strike. On the other hand, nothing is more frustrating than doing your best to get a take, while watching fish repeatedly feed on natural forage. The object of learning presentation casts is to analyze the situation and present the fly in a manner the fish will respond to with a strike. To have good presentation skills, an angler must not only master exact fly placement and line control, but also understand the application of a number of casts in real situations. The number of casts an angler needs to master depends on the technique, species, and location.

When selecting a presentation strategy, including cast selection, we should consider habitat and fish behavior in order to successfully catch fish in our chosen manner. For the purposes of this book, presentation casts will also include masking the angler's presence as manifested by the sight of our fly rods, lines, flies, and casting motion. What we do to manipulate the movement of the fly is more in the scope of fishing and not casting.

Reducing the casting distance to fish you target increases your accuracy and limits the problem of wind and drag in certain presentations. Where you position yourself is one of the most important basics in fishing or hunting, which are similar. Look at river current and pick the best spot to cast from and the best way to get there without spooking fish. Give thought to where and how you enter the water. When fishing for hard-to-approach fish, don't spook them with your vessel, silhouette, casting motion, reflection, shadow, waves, and anything else threatening to the fish. In many places, trout are habituated to humans or have had the wildness bred out of them and are easy to approach. Trout that rarely have human contact are totally intolerant of human presence. Inshore saltwater species have instincts that make them extremely shy in shallow water where they are vulnerable to predation.

When fish are spooky, use vegetation and topography to camouflage yourself on approach. Walk rod-rearward along the water so rod flash doesn't scare the fish. You may even have to approach your casting spot on hand and knees, like Bob Jacklin of West Yellowstone showed me on one of his favorite creeks crossing a pasture. In some places you might have to crawl as much as a hundred feet to avoid spooking fish. Instead of standing and walking down the bank to enter the stream, consider sitting down on a bank and swinging your legs into the water. Besides avoiding detection, remember to wade into a position for better drifts. I learned a counterintuitive approach in Idaho a few years ago from a local wearing a cowboy hat.

I was casting on an angle upstream to fish feeding along a cut-bank thirty feet away on Idaho's Henry's Fork. Suddenly I heard splashing about an eighth of a mile downstream and saw an angler in a cowboy hat wrangling a steelhead-sized trout. After he released it, the man waded upstream in my direction silhouetted by the bank and almost invisible to fish holding off the bank. He was using the bank as camouflage, had the ideal approach angle on the tail of big bank feeders, and had negligible drag on his upstream casts. He kindly exited and walked around me to avoid spooking my fish and reentered a polite distance upstream. I caught a few fish and he quietly waded ahead selecting big noses to cast to. He was only focused on the fish ahead, not the ones he spooked behind. Could be the lines for a Western song.

No matter what type of presentation you want to attempt, you first have to master your ability to place a fly exactly where you want it. Being able to determine where you want it, or picking an exact spot involves understanding your target species and its habits. You have to decide how quietly and close you need to present your fly without spooking the fish. You can sight-fish for individual fish or telltales, or entire schools, or fishing structure. You should pick a target wherever you cast. The foundation for good accuracy and presentation is faultless form and good loop control. Loop control isn't just the ability to make a tight loop, it's the ability to make any size loop, when you want to. Sometimes it's useful to make a wide loop. An angler can cast a wide loop to prevent tangling an unbalanced fly or split-shot rig, or to slow down turnover for a light lay down with slack. You also need to be able to cast at any speed and at any rod plane and combat the wind to achieve your goals.

FIELD TIP

When fishing a river, mark a shore point in your mind opposite a rising fish and also note its relation to any structure or fairly constant current signatures on the surface. Boulders, bars, or weed beds deflect water and show unique currents on the surface. That way, if you move, or the fish are down, you will still know where you last saw them.

ACCURACY

During heavy mayfly hatches, I swear, sometimes you have to cast a dry fly into a fish's mouth to hook it. Often it takes many casts. Some call it force-feeding. The fewer bugs on the water, the farther the fish are willing to swim to eat, and vice versa. I remember an example of excessive food on one afternoon in particular on the East Branch of the Delaware River during a green drake spinner fall; commonly called the coffin flies. A few green drakes were emerging and lots of spinners were in the air. When they fly by like the witches in *Wizard of OZ,* you never know when or if they're going to land. I stood in one spot for an hour and the fish were feeding heavily as the spinner-fall started and intensified. At the peak, I think there were a dozen of the 3-inch long insects per square foot. Some were ovipositing and others were dying or lying spent on the surface.

I was using a Dette-style coffin fly but the fish would only come up and nose it. The water was just too slow for it where I was fishing, but a line of anglers had rooted themselves at the faster head of the pool. As the light started diming, I changed to a parachute coffin I tied on a long-shank hook and moved toward the biggest rising fish I could reach without encroaching on the next angler. I estimated the fish at four pounds and the angler next to me was casting to a fish I know was about six pounds. My fish regularly lifted its head to feed and I kept casting, since she didn't seem to mind.

I continued casting again in the last light and reduced the drift length each time until I was casting inches from her chin, until I hooked her. After the fight and a blurry underwater photo, I saw the other angler trudge out of the water muttering in discouragement by the irony of his fishless night. When I got out and turned on my headlamp, I saw my waders were covered in green colored green drake eggs. It looked like green caviar and was hard to remove.

Good casting accuracy gives you the ability to place a fly where you want it, with little deviation from the effects of wind. When I refer to "target" in accuracy, it may be a real target or the spot we visualize on the water where we want the fly to land. It might be inches or yards away from a fish, shoal of fish, or a hiding place. If you can keep most casts within a 30-inch ring, up to fifty feet away, you have very good accuracy. I've invited instructors to cast at targets during ACA demos and even good casters have difficulties with finite accuracy. They would stop several feet above the target, as if casting to make a soft landing. Unfortunately, there is almost always some side wind to blow the fly off course.

Although tournament accuracy competitors need a strong lay-down, it is really helpful for some fishing applications too, especially in wind. Controlling the landing point of the fly requires three things. First, you must control the rod with adequate wrist and forearm strength to control side deviation of the rod if you use your wrist. If there is any angular motion at the last moment, the rod tip will curve outward and the leader will not lay down straight. The stroke, which means the path of the hand, must compensate for wind drift, too. Second, the aiming point must be close vertically to the target, so you don't get curved layout. Third, there must be enough line speed for complete leader straightening and minimal wind deviation. When it's windy, you're going to need to increase line speed with a faster stroke and by adding hauling.

After I began tournament casting in 2003, my friend Phil Beebe, who regularly took me night snook fishing in his skiff, said he was amazed at my increased accuracy in fishing. Casting at targets between trips for a couple of years enabled me to put the fly under docks and lights and catch plenty of snook.

Joan Wulff says if you're going to practice casting, you should use a target. It gives an aiming reference for the opposing backcast. In her books, she doesn't prescribe casting at hula or tournament hoops, but if you enroll at her school, you'll cast at tournament hoops in her ponds. If you first learn how to cast at targets, you'll be well equipped to use that skill in your fishing presentation. I'm not advocating a straight-line cast for all fishing presentations, but knowing how to make one will help when it comes to making slack line presentations.

Chris Korich taught me how to cast the ACA tournament fly accuracy games. He keeps his tournament tackle in a locker at the GGACC (Golden Gate Angling and Casting Club) and only takes it out two or three times a year to compete. He will usually shoot a few perfect scores in the accuracy events, which is extremely difficult to do. The first thing he taught me was the "free throw" stance, with the casting-side foot forward, in-line with the hip and shoulder. Next he showed me his efficient "side-of-body" casting arm alignment with a near vertical rod plane. As I detailed in the description of stroke mechanics, a near vertical rod plane will help prevent a curved, or tucked layout of the line and leader, which will likely miss the target. Having the casting hand to the side of your head enables visual triangulation of the target and fly. This helps judge the distance of the cast in relation to the target.

A comparison of the caster's perspective of aiming and triangulating in different casting planes.

Before you start casting, make sure your contact with the ground is solid and your body is balanced and relaxed. Notice the amount and direction of the wind. On the first casts at the target, lengthen the cast to adjust line length and hover the fly about five feet over it. Most casters aim for the back of the rim. You might need to use "Kentucky Windage" on the long targets in a side-wind. That is, to compensate by aiming upwind as much as necessary to hit the target, depending on the amount of wind. Hovering is an old tournament accuracy technique used to see the fly better while measuring and aiming. You hover the fly by casting with enough forward line speed so the fly isn't already falling before it stops. You must let the leader turn over and the fly will almost hang, or hover momentarily. According to Paul Arden, Tasmanian instructor Peter Hayes does it differently, " . . . he hauls on the backcast, casts forward with power, and 'gives' with the line hand on the turnover to hover the fly . . . " I understand he learned the technique from Rodney Foy, the Australian casting champion.

Next, after approximating the right casting length, you should pin the line to the grip with the index finger and either lengthen or shorten the line until the length looks exact. IFFF MCI and ACA tournament caster, Larry Allen, wrote on p.25 of the Fall 2007 issue of the IFFF newsletter, *The Loop*, "I notice that most good casters look up at their front stop and watch the forward loop develop and follow it down to the fly. Watching over the target is almost impossible, as the fly comes into the window of vision for only a fraction of a second." To make final adjustments, lower the forward cast approximately one foot at a time until the fly is hovered about one foot above the center of the target. A good backcast is essential to eliminate drop or wind deviation. The backcast should have a tight loop and be made strongly. When you lower the front trajectory you must raise the back, so they are 180 degrees opposed.

The last move is to "Cut the Cake." Center the rod, unrolling loop and fly, on a target on the lay-down. Visualizing it, you press down with a stiff wrist, like cutting a cake. The object is to get the leader to straighten completely, so the fly lands before the leader or line. This isn't a useless discipline. In fishing, this helps lengthen a dead drift, since it helps delay the line from bowing downstream.

To make a good laydown, a fast high backcast is required, or the unrolled leader can crash short of the target. You must aim so your leader unrolls inches above the target or wind will blow your fly out of the target. The laydown in Dry Fly and Trout Fly Accuracy casting games causes the fly to land harder than you'd typically desire while dry fly fishing for trout, but does ensure accurate placement. In a fishing situation, you'd aim a foot higher and the energy will be dissipated and the fly will land softly.

At one of my earlier ACA Nationals during my round of Bass Bug Accuracy, Steve Rajeff was the head judge on my station. I just wanted to get it over with since I hadn't practiced enough. Steve followed me off the dock saying, "You got some 'splainin' to do!" Since I was his last caster, he walked me back and said, on every one of your casts, your leader was across the center of the target but you were either a little long or short. All you had to do was measure the line between the targets with your hands, and you'd hit them! He was right. The targets are about six feet apart and you can use two small line strips or one huge one and shoot that amount into your cast at each successive target. Steve and most other seasoned tournament casters have learned to judge distance instinctively for most events.

It's fun and deadly to play with "measuring" if you know the right spacing. ACA has an old game called Wet Fly Accuracy that only allows a pick-up and laydown and requires measured strips to win. If your casting distance is off, use the cast as a reference and make the needed adjustment by releasing or strip-in for the next cast. You can perform a similar technique if you're drifting, swinging, or skating a fly on an imaginary grid for salmon or steelhead. You work your fly across the grid a foot at a time until you've got it covered. That way, every fish in the pool or run has seen your fly. My friend Topher Browne explains this technique in his brilliant book, *Atlantic Salmon Magic*, Wild River Press, 2011 p.119–123.

The science and psychology of aiming is interesting to investigate. Dr. Gordy Hill posed the question whether the amplitude of movement during aiming might be relative to the size of the target our mind perceives. The premise is that small adjustments are "steadier" than larger ones, therefore giving greater control over accuracy. Steve Rajeff said he imagines a mini-tornado spinning into the center of the target. With every false cast he makes lower and lower, his fly gets closer to the center of the target, until he makes his laydown. We all have a certain aiming point on our target during the hover. Steve says he aims for the back of the rim at our clubs with casting docks above the water. Jay Clark, a good tournament caster who grew up at the GGACC and has multiple IFFF instructor certifications, stated, "Hovering just over the front edge, works on flat ground. Just remember, if you cast from an elevated position, the higher you are, the 'deeper' or further back in the target you'll need to aim." [Sexyloops.com]

When you can carry sufficient length in the air and false cast to your target, you'll be more accurate than when shooting line. When you have to shoot some line, you control distance by sight and feel. As you shoot line through the fingers of your line hand, you watch the loop and fly approach the target, and have a couple of choices. You can let the cast "hit the reel," or come tight and turn over. If the amount of line you stripped off was exact, then good. If not, the cast will be short. Or, you can shoot line and feather its flight with finger pressure to slow or stop it where you want it, placing the fly on target.

Joan Wulff once told me, "Tournament casting teaches us what to expect of our tackle." You can speed up your accuracy learning curve by participating in ACA accuracy events yourself. No other casting strips down the stroke to its essentials better than casting at target rings. From the Catskills to the Pacific, sixteen ACA clubs and their members are ready to welcome you and share more than one hundred years of casting knowledge. Several of the clubs have concrete ponds with floating targets dedicated to casting. The three Official ACA Accuracy events are Trout Fly Accuracy, Dry Fly Accuracy, and Bass Bug Accuracy. The events have specific tackle rules and are usually cast with a 6-, 7-, and 9-weight rod, respectively. ACA also has three fly distance events. You can find ACA online at americancastingassoc.org.

STRAIGHT-LINE CASTS

In a straight-line cast, the line and leader unroll before or while landing on the water and there is no slack. It is the most accurate cast and most often used when fishing freshwater lakes and ponds or in saltwater. In these cases the flies are often retrieved to impart action. A straight-line cast also creates the least problems with wind and if you don't have slack between you and the fish, you might miss fewer strikes.

It is the basic cast for swinging, skating, and riffling presentations on running water too. You can add aerial or water mends after the cast for control. Remember, the amount of downstream angle will control depth and speed. If you're casting sinking flies, the casting angle in relation to the current will help determine how deep the fly sinks. Casting upstream will let it sink on the slack as it approaches but after it passes downstream of the angler, the fly will start accelerating and lifting on the swing. Swinging can be done with surface or subsurface flies. Your aiming point should be calculated so the fly is at the right depth when it reaches the fish's position.

If the fish you are targeting react more to a moving presentation, then you give the fly movement, or strip it, starting with a straight, tight line. Poppers and streamers usually require action and pauses to entice a strike. In a rip or current, an active presentation is achieved with a crosscurrent or quartering cast to maintain tension. When there is no slack, you can move the fly with the rod tip and the stripping hand. If the current causes a bow that makes it hard to give the fly life, you'll need to straighten the line with an upstream mend.

On the other hand, if drag causes rejection or puts rising fish down with dry flies, then slack is desirable for a drag-free presentation. This is also important for nymph fishing. When fishing running water you either make slack-line casts or add slack with on-the-water mends, after the cast is made. Feeding slack is very effective when trying to prevent drag casting to a fish directly downstream but requires care. John Goddard warned about fishing downstream in his book *Trout Fishing Techniques* (1996): " . . . you always have the problem of retrieving the fly line from below the trout without spooking him, often very difficult if you are forced to fish directly downstream to a trout." Casts for dealing with drag are covered on p. 58.

CHANGE-OF-DIRECTION CASTS

When you finish a swing or a drift in flowing water and want to reposition the fly upstream, it is best to make an easy, efficient change-of-direction cast. Change-of-direction casts are also required if you're trying to methodically fan-cast and cover stillwaters or saltwater. There are many choices of casts and some are more suitable for certain situations than others.

The most basic and tedious change-of-direction cast is the star cast. It is false casting incrementally in a circle until you've reached your desired change of direction. If you're not in a hurry and want to dry a fly in the process, you might use this one.

You can use water tension to intentionally load a rod to make a change-of-direction cast. If your fly is awash downstream and you want to make a short upstream cast, you can slowly accelerate the rod to load it against the resistance of the current on the line, leader, and fly. As the fly breaks the surface, you make the forward stroke. This is called a tension cast. This is the simplest way to make short casts with tandem rigs and heavy nymphs. If you want a safe, easy change of directions, you can use a Belgian cast. You would pick up the fly and aim it directly at your intended target, using the oval stroke to provide the change.

One of my favorite change-of-direction casts is the wye cast. You may not realize you are already using it. We often false cast to measure correct casting length to an imaginary target above where we want the fly to land, so we don't spook a fish. We then make a backcast opposite the intended landing point and make the presentation. This cast is described in *The Complete Science of Fly Fishing and Spinning,* by Frederick G. Shaw (1915). To make the wye cast, pick up the fly from downstream and turn your body in the direction of your target while making an oval backcast 180 degrees opposite your target. Let the backcast straighten, then make your delivery.

FIELD TIP

When your only option on a backcast is a hole in the trees or brush, make a Belgian cast back into the hole, then forward on the presentation as a change-of-direction cast.

If you don't adhere to the 180-degree principle, you can use the roll cast with relatively small changes of angle without consequences. When you want more change of angle than just a modified roll cast and you don't have backcast room, Spey casts are the best option. These include, but are not limited to: single-Spey, double-Spey, Snap-T, snake roll, etc.

The Galway is useful for making a cast with limited backcast room. The backcast is made into an opening between tree branches and the forward cast made across stream.

The Galway cast originating in Ireland, links two forward casts in different directions. There are at least three ways to use this cast but I'll only cover change of direction here. To perform the Galway, you must rotate the wrist between casting directions so the palm is always facing the casting direction. If you perform both casts in a straight line, it is a 180-degree change of angle cast. If you round the stroke and make it more elliptical, you can make changes as large as 90 degrees.

The prevailing wind along the New Jersey coast for most of the surf fishing season is Southwest. Since Barnegat Bay and its barrier islands lie North and South, a SW wind blows on the casting shoulder of all right-handed surfcasters. To cast in a stiff wind in this direction, anglers found that standing with the wind at their backs and delivering the fly with their backcast kept the danger of the hook away. This cast became known as the Barnegat Bay cast. World famous fly designer Bob Popovics is making this cast on page 88. It can be used as a wind cast and a change-of-direction cast. Like the Galway cast, it is best used to provide a 180-degree change of angle. The Barnegat Bay cast is really just a backcast but serves multiple purposes. Mark Sedotti of Port Chester, NY, has a long distance cast called the sayonara sling. He delivers large weighted flies using the backcast and the rod butt tight to his forearm.

SLACK LINE CASTS

Jason Borger, Gary's son and an accomplished fly fishing author and artist, told me the toughest place on earth to get drag free drifts with a dry fly is Idaho's Henry's Fork of the Snake River. It took me a while to take up the challenge and when I did, I was surprised by the hydraulic characteristics of the famous Harriman Ranch section. Instead of currents created by boulders and bottom contours as in most streams, profuse aquatic weeds cause most of the surface currents that produce the notorious drag. Fishing a dead-drift successfully under those conditions can be achieved, if you learn how.

Think of the waters you fish as a golf course. Select your tackle like a golfer chooses clubs. Choose where to stand to make your cast, where to place the fly, and the way you want the line to lay upon the water. It's like planning the roll of a putt on an uneven green. After the fly lands, keep track of its drift speed. Watch the rate the current consumes the slack, make adjustments, follow the fly with the rod tip, watch the fly as it disappears into the mouth of a fish, like a golf ball dropping into the cup!

The currents of a river often vary in speed and direction between you and the fish you're casting to. In these cases we're forced to use casting direction, line and leader layout, and slack to compensate. Depending on the speed differential of currents your line crosses, the fly will drift slower than the current or it will move faster. When the fly is going to drag or move faster than the current where it is drifting, you need to put slack upstream where your line crosses the fastest flow. If the slack is being consumed by the faster current without pulling on the leader, it buys time before dragging. If the fly is moving too slowly because of slower water holding it back, you might have to mend into a current to help it match the current speed. These maneuvers give the fly a natural drift for a few seconds, so the fish will hopefully hit it before the fly heads off like a water skier and sends the fish into hiding.

In John Judy's book, *Slack Line Strategies for Fly Fishing* (1994), he shared a profound slack-line concept. His Control Tension chapter describes a range of slack from too much, or fishing "soft" without control or the ability to even set the hook, to fishing relatively tight without a free and undisturbed drift, but having "hard" control. He urges us to work on increasing slack and fishing right on the edge of too much. Personally, I often see anglers use too much slack and miss hooking fish as a result. Also, it does little good if one makes noisy mends of any kind.

You can achieve slack in the fly line and leader in three ways. First, include it in the leader design, add slack during the cast and before landing, and, lastly, adjust the line position after the line lands and during the drift. Since this section is on slack line casts and I will cover leader construction and mends later, I'll describe the major slack line casts. The first are my Three P's: the Parachute, the Pile, and the Positive Curve. I realize the first two are influenced by speed and trajectory before the rod stop and formed with down mends by definition, so I hope no one minds the liberty.

The parachute cast adds slack but it is not delicate because of the height the line has to fall.

The parachute cast adds slack near the end of the fly line. You make a fairly high forward cast and stop it abruptly. When the loop opens, bring the rod tip back to near vertical. Then immediately follow the falling line to the water with the rod. Lowering the rod will add the slack and the line should lie in small "S" shapes.

A pile, or puddle cast adds a pile of slack line close to the angler. You can use it when the flow close to you is faster than where the rest of your line and fly is about to land and drift. It is also effective when made downstream to prevent drag. To create this pile of slack, aim your forward cast high and quickly lower your rod tip to the water's surface in front of you until the line and fly land. Another way to create slack in a similar manner is to make a wide loop cast and lower the tip. The object is for the leader to fall almost vertically and land with curves in it.

Curve casts have three main uses. You can use one to control the angle of presentation to an upstream fish, to lessen line drag by introducing slack, and lastly, to cast around obstacles and avoid lining fish. There are two curve casts: the positive curve, also called the overpowered curve, and the negative curve, or underpowered curve. The positive curve is a true curve and can actively cast around an object. Putting a negative curve around one is like pitching horse-shoes. Both are made during loop formation. These casts are often confused with mends, which are line manipulations after loop formation.

A postive curve cast is made sidearm or over the opposite shoulder, with the rod approximately 45 degrees or lower to the water. Overpower the cast and use an abrupt stop, then lower your rod tip toward the water. After the stop, the rod tip will rebound and form a curve opposite the curve of the loop of your cast. If you pull back about six inches after the stop, then reach forward and down with the rod tip to give line, an even more severe curve will form, resembling an L or J. This cast and mend combination is called the hook cast. If you want to make a longer positive curve cast, a haul will help accelerate the line. Dry a dry fly before making a curve cast or it will spray water toward your fish.

The positive curve cast, also known as the overpow-ered curve cast can help avoid obstacles and help make a fly first presentation in a few instances.

I made a memorable hook cast last year fishing with my friend Theodore Rogowski, a great conservationist and fly expert. I was standing in the middle of the river behind a big boulder watching occasional rises in the bubble stream when I noticed a big brown sipping next to another big boulder behind me. He kept it up and I knew there was only one way to get a fly over that fish without spooking it. I turned around and cast a hook above the rock, letting the fly arrive down the chute before the 14 foot leader. The fish struck and as I yelped in surprise, Ted saw it run upstream toward him around other boulders, then downstream past me like a bullet. After I reeled down on the fish, my clicker buzzed with a bent rod and in an instant the fly pulled out. It still made my day.

There are other ways of making curves, although they are actually aerial mends in combination with a cast. An aerial mend is made after the rod stop. The vertical curve I learned from Gordy Hill is used for right or left curves for right-handed casters. To make a curve to the left: starting with a near vertical rod, make a forward stroke with an inward wrist twist toward the face, and back out to the reel forward position. To make a curve to the right starting with a near vertical rod position and the reel facing rearward: Make a backhand stroke with an outward wrist twist to the front back, ending with the reel facing rearward. After Gordy and I performed all the curves and mends, he shared a story coincidentally related to curves.

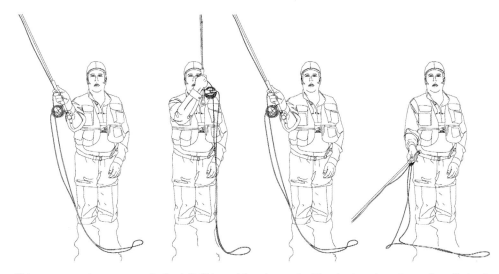

This sequence shows a curve to the left. This cast is only practical for short casts and uses the offset axis of the rod and the snapping motion to make the curve.

I asked Gordy, a long time friend of Lefty Kreh, what Lefty was like on fishing trips. Gordy said one time he and Lefty were on a freighter on their way to Africa and were getting bored. So Lefty and Gordy had a little casting contest to see who could hang out over the side and make curve casts into the portals along the side. Gordy said they both had fun but didn't keep score.

At the IFFF Conclave a number of years, back Jason Borger taught me another pseudo-curve named the corkscrew curve, originated by Bob Petzl, as described in an article, "Corkscrew Curve Cast," Gary A. Borger and Bob Petzl, *Fly Fisherman Magazine* May/June 1980. The cast starts with an overpowered stroke, then changes directions and repositions the line leg in the air with an aerial snap. It's fine to use it

The corkscrew curve is a combination of snaps and aerial mends to create a curved layout in the line. These moves should be made quickly before the line lands.

to avoid lining fish or to cast over a boulder. I use it from time to time. The rod starting position is nearly upright and the stroke is started on an angle aimed inward and down, then

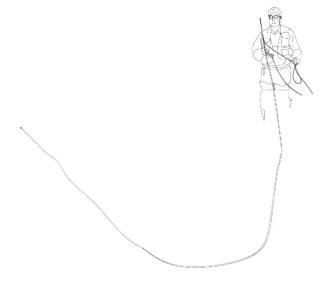

the stroke continues in a small clockwise semicircle to a stop. This cast can be made with good line speed and hauls to remarkable distances.

The negative curve, or under-powered curve, is a cast with an intentionally unopened loop, with-out turnover. You can use it for some similar purposes as the posi-tive curve, but it has less power and distance. The end of the line will not reach around a bank as an overpow-ered curve can. It is not well suited for use in wind as it is inaccurate and relatively slow.

The negative curve, also called an underpowered curve, is a cast you will seldom require but should have in your bag when you need it.

You make this cast by using a low rod angle side-cast, cross-body or back-hand cast. Make a medium to wide loop but you don't stop the rod until the fly, leader, and line have landed on the water. Slipping line also helps prevent turnover. You can gain some extra distance if you raise your rod hand slightly at the end of the cast. Stopping the rod as in a normal cast, would make the loop open. Reaching across the front of the body as the negative curve lands increases curve size.

The tuck cast makes the end of the fly line and leader curve down, making the fly and lead-ers land before the line. This cast helps the fly sink faster and gives it a little slack to do so. It can even be considered a vertical overpowered curve and it gets some assistance from gravity. Make the tuck cast with a fairly upright rod angle, otherwise, the cast will curve. Start with a low backcast and make the forward cast with extra speed and stop the rod at a 45 degrees angle.

The forward stop should be made abruptly so the end of the line kicks down. After the stop, drop the rod tip to follow the line downward, permitting the fly and leader to sink before the line lands. The tuck cast was intended for stream nymphing but works well in saltwater appli-cations with clousers and other weighted flies too.

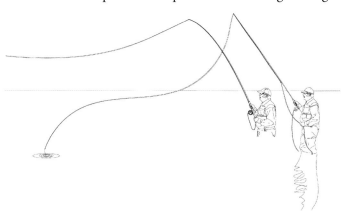

The tuck cast is essential for the nymph fisherman. The heavier the fly, the more it will kick into a vertical entry.

Englishman Frank Sawyer, most famous for creating the Pheasant Tail Nymph, was the first author to describe this technique, unnamed at the time, on p. 98–99 of his book, *Nymphs and the Trout* (1958). In *Techniques of Trout Fishing and Fly Tying* (1990), George W. Harvey describes the same technique and takes credit for it, "I call this cast the tuck cast and it is the most important fundamental one should learn when fishing in pocket or riffly water . . . As far as I know, I was the first to introduce this casting technique and the best nymph fishermen I know use it." Some say George Harvey and Frank Sawyer both created the cast at approximately the same time on two different continents.

MENDS

A mend is a line manipulation made after loop formation that creates or fixes the layout of a cast to avoid a fish or obstacle or to improve the drift of the fly line. Generally, if you make a mend upstream, it delays line drag by slowing speed; if it's made downstream, it increases drag and subsequently drift speed. An upstream mend also helps sinking lines and flies sink because of the decrease in drift speed.

There are two types of mends: aerial mends, those made before the line lands on the water; and water mends, those made after the line lands on the water. It is preferable to make an aerial mend instead of a water mend because it doesn't require the additional disturbance or the risk of accidentally jerking the fly on a dead drift. Water mends reposition line after the cast and at any time you wish during the drift. You would usually mend the line upstream to take the "bow" out, reduce drift speed and reduce drag when fishing dry flies. The most useful water mend starts by lifting some line off the water, without disturbing the fly, and flipping it gently upstream. On the other hand, if you are drifting a subsurface fly, a downstream mend will help increase drift speed, maintain tension, and help you hook the fish. When you use a downstream bow or belly, you can regulate the speed by the amount of downstream leading you do with your rod tip. You can also shoot or feed slack into the mend to increase its size. I'll first discuss the aerial mends, then the water mends.

The three most important aerial mends are the reach mend, S-mend and the curved mend. The reach mend is an easy technique to execute that lessens the angle of the line to help reduce drag. The instant your forward cast is on its way to your target, simply reach your rod tip 90 degrees upstream of your cast, ending with the rod tip just off the water's surface. Then follow the drift with the rod tip and the angle of the line on the water will increase slowly until the fly drags. This has increased the length and duration of drag-free drift. Think of it geometrically. The shortest distance between two points is a straight line, or in this case a straight line cast. By performing this mend, you make an imaginary triangle between you and the target, the rod tip, and the line of your casting arm and the rod.

The lesser angle and extra line make this an invaluable technique. You can also use this mend to prevent lining a fish between you and a fish you're casting to. This is especially helpful if the fish you're casting to is directly up or downstream of your casting position. Lastly, my friend NYS Guide and IFFF MCI, Craig Buckbee, confided recently he makes downstream reach mends with streamers to maintain good tension during a swing.

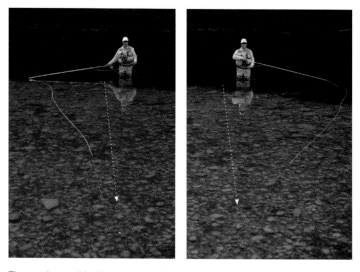

The S-mend lands on the water with snakelike curves in the line. The curves are slack and delay the drag of the current on an otherwise straight line. You make this shape by wiggling the rod tip side-to-side after loop forma-tion. The width, or amplitude,

The reach mend is the most practical way to prevent drag. When you need to make it on the opposite of your casting side, reach across your body to make the mend.

of the resulting wiggle in the line on the water is determined by the width of the rod motion forming them. To accurately place your fly, land it first by slightly delaying the sideways rod wiggle. This will not add a curved layout to the leader. The next most important aerial mend is the curved mend.

A curved mend is a curve placed in the line after loop formation to add slack, tension, or to avoid a fish or obstacle and more. To add slack to a dead drift to prevent drag, make the curve upstream where the cast crosses the fastest current. The time it takes for the current to consume the slack extends the length of drag-free drift. You make this mend by quickly moving the rod hand in the direction you want the mend, then quickly returning it back to the starting position.

The timing of this movement determines the placement of the curve along the length of the cast. The width of the movement determines the width, or amplitude of the curve. So, if you want the curve near the leader, you move the rod as fast as possible after the rod stop in your forward cast. If you want it in the middle, you delay until at least the leader lands. If you want the curve under the rod tip, you wait until about half of the line has landed on the

The S-mend is one of the most effective ways to minimize drag. To make the "S" in larger amplitude, move the rod hand from side to side instead of just wiggling the rod tip.

water. If you make the mend downstream, it will increase tension in the line. If you make a cast quartering downstream near a bank and throw a curved mend near the fly aimed toward the bank, the fly will swim toward the bank when the line straightens at the end of the drift.

You make a water mend after the cast has landed on the water and you have to pick up line off the water in order to reposition it. A simple water mend is used to position a curved portion of line for speed control and avoid drag. To avoid drag, make an upstream mend to slow the drift. When the fly is drifting too slow, make a downstream mend or place a portion of the line on a faster current. Making a downstream mend is common way to maintain tension when drifting a subsurface fly from a driftboat.

The hump mend is another useful water mend. You prepare for this cast by having coils of line between the fingers of your line hand and a low rod tip pointed at the fly. Start this water mend by vertically bouncing and loading the rod tip while letting line slip out through your fingers and onto the water. The slack lands in waves proportional to the size of the mend. I use it for feeding line to extend a drift downstream beyond the length of a practical cast. This is also a way to get a fly under an overhang. Often times, I don't have backcast clearance or can't rock while wading to make an 80-foot cast with a 4-weight, so instead I feed line with a hump mend. I make small hump mends after the downstream cast lands, so the line is almost tight as I feed it and can promptly set the hook. Some anglers use a pile or other slack cast downstream to lengthen the drift and by so doing, miss strikes.

With the curved mend, you can target where you put the slack in order to control the drift speed. It is preferable to use one instead of a water mend because it disturbs the water less.

The stack mend is similar to the hump mend except the stroke is side to side. You would generally make a short cast then stack a pile of slack to help a sinking fly line sink better in salt or stillwaters. I've used this to reach bottom in forty-five feet of water and caught fish.

The roll cast mend is sort of a hybrid water mend and used similarly to the hump mend. It's a roll cast and a shoot made during a drift without moving the fly. It adds slack to prevent drag, or lengthen the drift. If you want to cast across a wide current without drag, make the cast then roll cast a loop of slack one or more times downstream as close to the rod tip as possible and it will delay the line coming tight and dragging. You can do the same maneuver before a downstream presentation comes tight and extend the drift.

When I was fishing with Paul Arden in Croatia, he introduced me to Aleksandar Puskadija, (a.k.a. Sasha) Balkans nymph expert and EFFA Basic Instructor. Sasha taught me how to control nymph drift speed when using a long-line presentation. He showed me to cast upstream and then make an on-the-water mend downstream to make a loop in the line that acts like a sea anchor. The size of loop in the mend and how you regulate its size during the drift controls the drift speed. A larger loop shows the effects of current drag and speeds up, a smaller loop drags less and slows the drift. This speed also affects fly depth. The slower it goes, the deeper.

As I said in the introduction, almost everything taught today in fly casting was developed in the nineteenth and early twentieth centuries. Most techniques evolved for salmon and sea trout fishing and are very useful for other species and places as well. The first written description of a mend before it was even named can be found in H. Cholmondeley-Pennell, Vol. I *Fishing, Salmon and Trout* (1885), quoting Major John P. Traherne:

> There is a way of taking the belly out of a line, which was taught me by an old fisherman when fishing the Kirkcudbrightshire Dee in my younger days. I dare say many of my readers will recollect old Jemmy Gordon . . . It was Jemmie that pointed out to me the evil of allowing a belly to remain in my line, and who taught me how to rectify it . . . By making a back-handed upward cast, the belly, the outward curve of which is facing down stream, is changed in its direction . . . the outward curve facing up stream . . . the fly will then work gradually across stream, the rod following the fly until the cast is competed . . .

Traherne's drawing in the text illustrates various types of manipulations which were later called mends, since they repaired the line layout. John Alden Knight calls them mends in his 1942 book, *Modern Fly Casting*.

FIELD TIP

Lane change—When a fly starts to drag, you can reposition it closer by skittering it across the current for a new drift initially without drag. An upstream mend after this maneuver also helps. Angler and author John Judy calls this the Skitter and Drop, p. 61 *Slack Line Strategies for Fly Fishing* (1994).

WIND CASTS

Sometimes the best fishing is during the worst weather. Predatory fish feel safer feeding under the cover of clouds and surface disturbance. This means windy conditions, with various types of precipitation possible. When you're casting out in the open, wind is a challenge to all elements of performance and pleasure. I'm often asked about under-lining and over-lining a rod to deal with wind. I almost always cast what I determine to be a balanced line and rod combination for maximum distance. On a blue moon, I might over-line a rod if I'm only casting less than a whole 30-foot head, as when fishing in tiny trout streams. As I cover in detail in the equipment section, when there is wind, I will use a faster action rod of the same line weight, or jump up a size with the whole outfit. For example, for trout I'll go up from a 4-weight outfit to a 5, or for adult tarpon, from an 11-weight outfit to a stiff 12. A heavier line cast at the same speed as a lighter one will be more effective at overcoming the wind. But even with the right gear, it's all in the technique.

If wind is blowing onto the same side as your line hand, it's not much of a problem. It will probably suffice to use additional line speed to prevent wind drift on your line and fly to maintain distance and accuracy. Wind on your casting shoulder is a potential hazard because the fly and line can hit you. If the wind is light, maybe 5 mph, additional line speed will again help. If it's puffing 5-10 mph, I recommend a fast, low side-arm stroke.

The first defense against a breeze on your casting shoulder is a low sidearm cast as shown.

This will separate you and the hook by almost a rod length and if the loop is a little wobbly on the backcast, it'll hit the water, instead of a person or the boat. When it's blowing 10–15 mph, I recommend the off-shoulder and cross-body cast. If it's blowing 15–25 mph, I recommend the Barnegat Bay cast for safety and comfort. At least the wind will be at your back! Another way to deal with wind on your casting side is to use your non-dominant hand. Remember, wind is seldom constant, use any break between gusts or favorable change in angle, to make a better cast.

To make the right-handed off-shoulder cast, angle the casting plane to the left overhead by lifting the elbow, with the casting hand stopping above the right ear. This places the rod tip and path of the line and fly, downwind, out past the left shoulder. Move the line hand outward so the line is not in your face. You will be looking through the opening between the line and the rod like looking through a window. The cross body cast operates on a similar principle but the stroke arc is either in front of the chest or outboard of the left shoulder if you need to make a longer stroke. This cast requires extension and retraction of the arm to keep the rod tracking straight. That covers two of the four wind directions. Casting with a tailwind and into a headwind are still ahead.

When you're casting with a tailwind or downwind and the wind is at your back, it will help carry your forward cast but unfortunately the wind will put the brakes on your backcast. Angle your backcast downward to reduce lift and angle the forward correspondingly upward. The wind will help carry and open the forward cast. False casting with the wind can cause excessive line speed like a bullwhip and overly abrupt stops. It should be done with reduced stroke and hauling effort to prevent problems.

This shows an off-shoulder cast with the line hand located so the line isn't in your face.

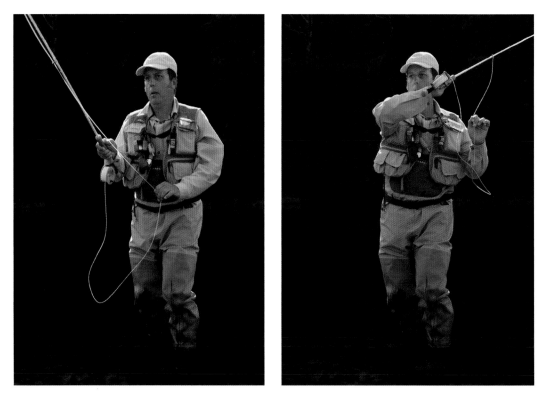

The cross body cast used to keep the line and fly downwind for safety, maintains the normal stroke and uninterrupted vision. In compromise, this cast reduces distance potential.

If you're casting into a headwind, direct your forward cast as close to the water as possible and direct your backcast on an upward trajectory 180 degrees away from the forward cast. Presenting close to the surface prevents excessive wind drift. In addition, when casting against the wind, use adequate line speed by making a harder stroke and/or, a faster double-haul. A headwind will have an affect on backcast timing because loops open faster down wind, but may stay aloft longer due to wind drag. Remember, shooting line downwind in a false cast might overload the rod when casting in the other direction into the headwind. This will cause a wide loop and lost line speed. Also, refrain from shooting too much line into the backcast against the wind or it can stall.

When the wind is howling and you're wading in the open, try using very low sidearm casts with a downwind delivery. By casting as close to the water as possible without touching it with the fly or line, you take advantage of four things. First, by reducing casting angle, you are reducing the frontal area of the line. Second, there is a slight differences in the wind speed closer to the surface of the water than higher above. This wind speed gradient was featured in Larry Pratt's article, *Under the Wind,* in the Spring 2001 issue of *The Loop.* The third thing is, the wind will assist in loop and leader turnover. Even if you don't get good backcast turnover, the force of the wind will straighten that forward cast right out! And lastly, the sidearm position almost assures the fly will not snag you. If the wind is blowing downstream, consider a downstream presenta-

tion. If it's upstream, consider an upstream presentation. Does that suggest to always pick a downwind cast when the wind is howling? Maybe so. I also recently learned a new wind cast from my newest Island friend.

At the Fly Fishing Show in Marlborough in 2013, I was trying to make a connection with Tourism Bahamas for my Flats Prep School, when I met Prescott Smith, owner of Stafford Creek Lodge, Andros Island, Bahamas. He is a great guide and son of Charlie Smith, originator of the Crazy Charlie. When I told him I prepare northern anglers for the ravages of the windy flats, he told me he developed a technique he calls Taming the Wind. He even put out a DVD about it. He told me the way most people cast in wind is wrong. He shuns tight loops when casting into the wind because he says stopping the rod makes the line more susceptible to the wind.

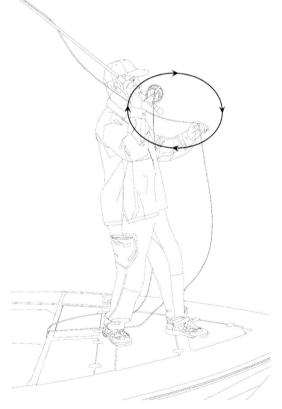

"Taming the Wind" uses constant motion to prevent the wind from ruining a cast on the flats.

We went to the casting pool without any wind and he demonstrated his technique. Prescott made an overhead cast with an oval stroke without stopping the rod or the line. He used a medium size loop with constant tension until the delivery stop. After the stop, he quickly lowered his rod tip and elevated the rod butt by raising his elbow. This anchored the line in the rod leg of the line in the water to prevent wind drift. This technique does not let the line slow enough for gravity or wind to really affect the cast. Prescott's favorite way to deal with wind on his casting side is the "over the opposite shoulder cast." For most people the Taming the Wind Cast is limited to a maximum of about sixty feet, but on a really windy day, many anglers will take that!

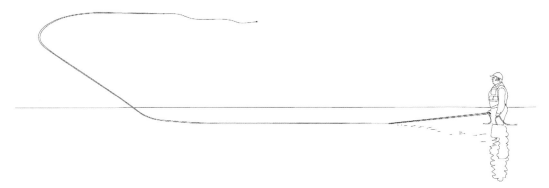

The Mulson cast, also known as the Madison cast, uses a mend down to the water after the stop to minimize the wind's influence on the rod leg of the cast.

The finish of Prescott's cast reminded me of Chris Korich's laydown in ACA fly accuracy on a windy day. Chris says it's like the anchored line is a railroad track to the target. I know casters have been doing that trick for decades. A fishing cast was recently developed in parallel by a Florida angler named Joe Mulson and named after him as the Mulson wind cast. It can be described as a high-speed cast with a tight-looped cast with a down mend. The loop looks like the outline of a boat hull. Once the line touches, the wind has no affect over that portion and the energy transfers down the line until it straightens. In Montana, they have a similar cast they call the Madison cast, useful for casting in its notorious winds. Practice these casts under actual wind conditions at home before testing them on the flats.

THE SALTWATER QUICK CAST

Whether you're sight fishing while on shore, wading, or standing on the deck of a flats skiff, you must have the advantage of surprise. You must be able to quickly make long, accurate casts so neither you nor the boat you're in spook fish. When permit, tarpon, and bonefish are spooked, they will leave in a hurry and possibly alert other fish they encounter on their exit.

An experienced and considerate captain will always try to push the boat into a favorable angle for visibility and to cast at a fish. Many times though, that is not possible. He will call out the location of the fish using the numbers on a clockface and other instructions. The reference for the center of this clock is the center of the casting deck or platform on the bow. Ideally casts should be made at 10:00 or 11:00 for a right-hander. This provides the least chance of detection by the fish, an opportunity to adjust the boat angle, and the possibility of multiple shots. Fish that intercept the boat will spook from it. Fish approaching from this caster's right will often require a backhand cast. If the fish is at 12:00, present with a sidearm cast that won't hit the guide on the poling platform at 6:00! Or, if there is time and it won't spook the fish, the guide can push the boat into a safe casting angle with the bow facing 2:00.

The clock orientation on the front deck of a flats skiff used between angler and guide to communicate the location of fish and other features.

The saltwater quick cast helps the angler organize equipment in a state of readiness to minimize the time to safely and accurately present the fly. The object is to present the fly with the minimum number of false casts in order to load the rod, extend, and shoot the line. The first thing in the order of actually performing this cast is to consider the running line. It has to be ready to flow smoothly through your hands and guides. If it won't, it will blow the shot.

Your fly line must be absolutely clean and in good condition. Additionally, all line connections must be minimal so they will not catch in the guides. I recommend washing fly lines in warm soapy water every three days of use. I also carry a terry facecloth and some fresh water onboard to run a line through if I feel dried salt on it. Even if a manufacturer states their line has built-in lubricant, I'll clean and apply Glide line cleaner and lubricant at night, instead of socializing. I'll let it dry overnight and in the morning I'll buff the line with a dry terry and reel it up, ready to go.

If you're fishing on an elevated bow casting platform or staked out alone standing on the poling platform, a FlyLine Tamer (or the equivalent) is a helpful aid. Place one right in front of you on the platform. If you're going to fish from the bow deck, putting the line in the cockpit places it out of the wind and away from your casting area. I hate it when it blows off the deck and into the water. Even though the coils won't be directly under the rod guides in the cockpit, I've never had trouble shooting the line. I prefer a clean uncluttered deck and cockpit, so I do a little housekeeping before stripping out line. When I'm ready to fish in a skiff in warm weather, I take off my sandals or deck shoes and go barefoot. This way, I can feel any line beneath my feet. I strip out about eighty feet of line and stretch all of it between my hands and lay it on the deck. I

Line baskets are useful to organize line to keep it off the deck and protected from wind and waves. An angler can use small ones at waist level or large ones placed on the deck or platform.

then make a clearing cast. That's when you cast it out and strip it in. This is my recommended procedure for putting the line in the cockpit.

I carefully make the largest coils I can in the left side of the cockpit behind the casting platform. If you only strip line off the reel and onto the deck, the coils will be in the incorrect order for a cast. It will pull from the bottom up and tangle, instead of pulling from the top down. I stop arranging the coils of line with about two rod lengths of line, plus the leader, extended past the rod tip. I hold the fly hook by the bend between the index and thumb of my line hand with the point facing away. This is for safety. Control the line leading up to your stripping guide with the index finger of the rod hand. You can now shake another rod length of line out of the rod tip, so the large loop of line just grazes the water. You will have about twenty feet of fly line ready to begin the saltwater quick cast. The following description is for your longest cast. You might not need as many false casts or hauls for a close cast.

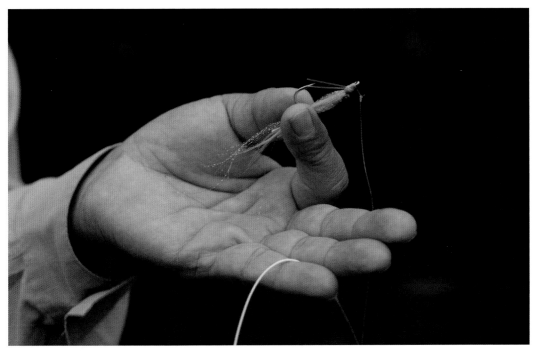

The safest way to hold a fly ready for a quick cast while sight fishing. Note how the line-leader connection is held with leader doubled as suggested in the field tip.

FIELD TIP

Double the leader for the saltwater quick cast and place the leader line junction between the little finger and the ring finger of the same hand. This trick helps load the rod quicker and might save one false cast.

The first cast depends upon the wind direction. Wind blowing in the direction of the cast helps straighten the line and load the rod, wind blowing against it will cause resistance. If the wind is in your face, start with a backcast and hold the hook away at an angle so the wind won't swing it into you. If the wind is behind you, start with a forward overhead cast or a roll cast. Let the cast pull the hook out and away from the fingers of your line hand and let the wind straighten the line and leader. If you wish, you can even let the fly anchor briefly to waterload casts. Double haul and shoot as much line as possible on two to three false casts and release the presentation cast. Make sure to maintain high line speed and no slack. If your fly hits the water during false casts, try shooting less line, raise the trajectory, or shorten your pause. You can even use your backcast for the delivery. The backcast is also the best way to cast to a fish on your rod side, especially if it's a close shot.

One mistake many new anglers make is lowering the rod to make their stop on the presentation cast, instead of making the forward stroke longer and maybe slightly higher in trajectory than the last false cast, then lowering the tip. I watch anglers false cast on my skiff and everything looks great until they make the last cast. I sometimes say when they're false casting, just let the next one go. The saltwater quick cast can also be used when sight fishing for striped bass, sharks, redfish, carp, trout, etc.

I've developed a workshop for practicing guide/angler communications and quickly casting to a radio-controlled fish on an indoor or outdoor field. I use the casting platform from my skiff and a six-foot platform ladder to simulate the relation and perspective from a full flats skiff. If you can't drill with a coach, practice at home and in the wind before you make your first trip and before each season for maintenance.

If you're wading on the flats or in the surf or casting from shore features like rock or jetty, a stripping basket will take the place of the boat cockpit in helping protect and arrange your line. I like the Orvis stripping basket, but still have my old Rubbermaid wash basin and bungee cord I keep in my flats skiff. If I need to anchor and fish off the stern, or I have a guest

I use a remote control fish, a casting and poling platform on dry land to teach first time flats anglers about communicating and casting before their first journey.

on the bow, I use my stripping basket. I can even run around the gunwale with my rod in hand to attend to something without tangling.

On the other hand, if you wade in rivers or streams and you make long casts, you probably wouldn't want a basket, since it'll float up on your body. If you make one that water can flow through, floating line can float about in it and foul, just like on a swamped deck, as I found out. In this case, holding coils of line in the line hand will work best. The way to arrange the coils is to strip in and coil six feet of line and hold it between the last too fingers of the line hand. This one should touch the water so tension prevents it from fouling on the way up the guides. Some call this the river loop. The next loop, slightly smaller goes between the next set of fingers until you are holding four coils in descending size. When you shoot the line, release each loop by reducing the pressure in each set of fingers until the cast is away. Hopefully it doesn't foul.

Billfishing with the bait-and-switch method requires as much readiness as flats fishing. It entails trolling hookless teasers and substituting a fly for the teaser at the moment you yank it away from a pursuing billfish. I like being the tease with my Cam Sigler Teaser Rod and Daisy Chains. The line runs through the blank to prevent it from wrapping on the guides, but even if the line wraps on the blank, you can just submerge it and the line usually slides off.

Organizing the fly tackle for bait-and-switch requires a FlyLine Tamer (or the equivalent) in the corner of the stern of a sportfisher or center console. The Line Tamer's location should enable you to have your casting arm pointing outward and casting parallel to the beam. Usually you would not use an outrig-

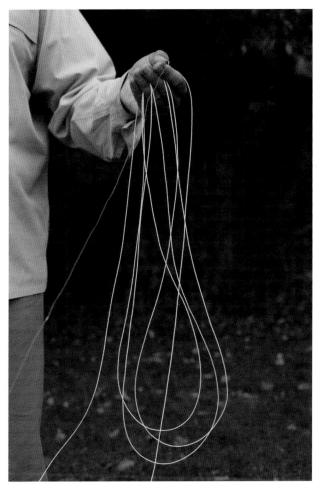

Holding line coils when wading is one way to make long casts without the pull of current on the line and tangling.

ger on that side to provide casting room. You will have only as much line in the FlyLine Tamer as you need for cast. That might be only the head plus forty feet of running line. Hang the fly on the stripper guide and hold the line to the rod with a Velcro strap so the wind and vibration don't let the line spill into the water. When an appropriately-sized billfish appears behind a teaser, grab the fly by the bend of the tail hook if it's a tandem, and release the strap holding the line. When the mate pulls the teaser away from the fish and the captain puts the motors in neutral, safely make your cast aiming just beyond and slightly outside of the fish to avoid lining it. The fish will usually turn around toward the sound of the fly and bite it going away. If it does, the hook will hopefully stick in the corner of the fish's mouth. Even though the boat is in neutral, it should continue forward momentarily at enough speed to keep your line high and taut. If the fish doesn't strike, strip until the fish strikes or the captain puts the boat in gear and the teaser is replaced. If you really want to satisfy a compulsion for this kind of fishing, contact Captain Jake Jordan at JakeJordan.com. He runs billfish schools in the Caribbean and elsewhere. Refer to the section on casting heavy outfits for more tips.

CASTS FOR LIMITED ROOM

Obstacles behind you like rock formations, a bank, or brush sometimes prevent making a regular backcast. The roll cast is the first choice to use to deal with this, but if fast water is in front of you or you're using dry flies, a steeple cast is the better choice. You will be able to false cast and if you can live with a short cast, it's preferable. Begin with your rod tip close to the water and the palm of the casting hand and reel facing up. Start an oval sidearm backcast rearward, stop the rod when the rod tip is straight up over your casting shoulder and your hand is just over your head. Your forearm will be vertical with your palm facing forward. Allow the loop to unroll overhead. Then make the forward stroke and stop the rod at a position so the cast has enough speed to unroll without tailing.

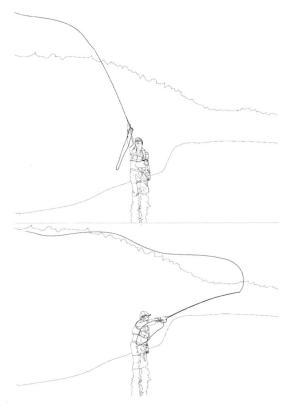

The steeple cast is used when you have limited backcast room but because it requires breaking the 180-degree rule, it is a tailing loop waiting to happen.

FIELD TIP

If you elevate the spiral as you do it, you can make a vertical spiral pick-up cast I learned from the late English angler, John Goddard. It forms a high, compact backcast, for when you have no room behind you.

The pendulum cast has an upside down loop and works for casting under brush in small streams or saltwater mangrove. The fly rides underneath, so it has a tendency not to snag if the loop doesn't quite fit under the overhang. To make this cast, use a sidearm cast with a saucer shaped forward stroke. The shallower the saucer, the tighter the resulting loop. According to Paul Arden, this cast can also be used to prevent line collisions when performing slack line roll casts.

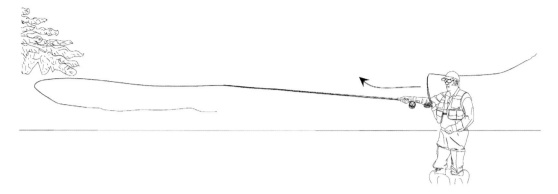

The pendulum cast, or underslung loop, prevents snagging when casting under brush but doesn't have a low enough profile unless you cast it sidearm.

Sometimes you have to improvise to cast your way out of a situation. A few years ago, I was wading along a steep riverbank on Connecticut's Farmington watching fish rise. I couldn't make a backcast so I decided to figure out some way to make the presentation. The river was flowing right and the wind was blowing upstream. I ruled out using a roll cast with a dry fly, since it would get waterlogged. False casting horizontally up and downstream, I slipped enough line for the cast. I made an oval forward cast and a haul at an angle upstream, continuing into a reach mend left on delivery. The angle of the mended line acted like a sail and gained extra distance from the wind. The cast gave my fly a good drift. This cast can also be made downstream, as long as the wind assists. When making this cast to the right, I would use an off-hand cast, or cast with the other hand. In Joan Wulff's book, *Joan Wulff's New Fly-Casting Techniques* (2012) she says when there is no backcast space, use the space above the water.

The Bow-and-Arrow Cast is useful when you have space limits everywhere on your casting, except directly ahead. You make this cast by holding the fly or tippet and loading the rod like the limbs of a longbow. Aim it like a slingshot. Your cast is limited by rod length, which on small streams where this cast is helpful, is usually around seven feet long. You can increase the distance by palming a coil of fly line in your fly hand. Here's a technique passed down by George Harvey to extend your reach.

The first step is to hold your rod under your casting arm to temporarily free your rod hand. Begin gathering line by making a loop of leader over the top of the

The bow-and-arrow cast is a stealthy cast for small waters with cast restrictions or when standing and revealing your silhouette would end the hunt.

index finger of your line hand, leaving the fly hanging about a foot below. Then pinch the leader between your index finger and thumb with the other fingers open. Close your line hand pinkie until it catches the leader going toward the rod tip. Use your rod hand and wrap loops of leader in the line hand index and pinkie like a leader holder until you have enough length to reach your target. Close the index finger of the line hand and lock the loops into the palm with the control of the line between the sides of the pads of the thumb pressed against the side of the index.

There should be no slack between the rod tip and the loops in the line hand when they are held even with the front of the grip. Now pinch the fly line to the grip with the index finger of the line hand and point the rod tip toward the target. Rotate your line hand forward until the line to the rod tip is trapped under all the fingers and is coming out from under the pinkie. With the thumb on top, load the rod by pulling the line back from the rod tip with the line hand and stop when it is near ear level and about a foot away, so the loops won't catch you. Aim at your target by aligning the line hand, rod tip, and target. To cast, release the loops first, then let the rod pull the tippet and fly safely out of your grasp. I recommend practicing this on the lawn first.

CASTING HEAVY FLIES AND LINES

Casting weighted flies and lines takes some special care. High-density lines matched for a given rod can be cast with a tight loop, with practice. I use a lot of large flies on New England rips and rely mainly on the weight of the line to sink them. I think a lighter fly is livelier in those situations. If I use a fly, or fly and weight combination that doesn't balance well and hinges, a larger slow loop helps prevent collisions. Since I finish my distance casts with a thrust, I realized it was making the flies enter first, like a tuck cast and helping them sink faster. The heavier the fly, the more it will kick. I have a heavy saltwater fly I tied and named Bunker Buster, after the ordnance used in Operation Desert Storm. When I cast this fly with a tight loop and stop it hard, it looks like a bomb falling.

The problem with casting sinking lines and flies, is getting them to the surface to recast. You can strip them all the way back or make one or more roll casts to help bring the fly to the surface for a pick up. Water loading can also shorten the process of getting the line back out and into a backcast. Using an oval cast will help prevent the fly from striking you or the rod.

NON-DOMINANT HAND

No matter whether you're trying to make overhead casts, rolls, or Speys with a one-hand rod, there are always times you wished you could use your other arm to cast with. The most opportune is when the wind is on your casting side. Another is when you need to rest your dominant hand or have an injury. I like practicing casting with my non-dominant hand inbetween trips with an indoor practice rod. Practice casting with a rod in each hand, so the dominant side can "teach" the non-dominant side.

FIELD TIP

To better learn non-dominant hand casting, have a friend stand next to your non-dominant side, both holding outfits without any line extended. Have her cast while you try to mimic the stroke together. If you're practicing lefty and she's demonstrating righty, your arms will be quite close making it easy for you to copy. If that looks smooth, take a few steps away sideways and both cast parallel together with twenty feet of line out. The stroke is usually easy; the pause is more difficult.

When you're prepared and confident, it will help you succeed and enjoy the experience all the more. Learning as much about the fish and their forage and figuring how to effectively present your fly is the greatest challenge in fly fishing. It's what connects you to the fish as a hunter. The process should be rewarding and the strike a validation. After a lifetime of catching fish, I like catching them but only when it's a challenge and the rewards are above average. When you figure out a presentation that never occurred to anyone else for a difficult spot, you have a secret spot with bigger, less-pressured fish than in the easier, overcrowded spots.

Side by side casting is an effective learning method because mimicking is an instinct. Here I show how you can learn to cast with a non-dominant hand by doing it closely with someone else's dominant hand cast.

CHAPTER 5

PRESENTATION SCENARIOS

L earning how to perform the various presentation casts in this chapter on your lawn will not adequately prepare you for their application in fishing situations afield. Therefore, I would like you to read the following examples, or fishing scenarios, and visualize similar places you fish and how you might use one of the casts in this chapter to make a good presentation to a big, wary fish.

FAST TO SLOW CURRENT

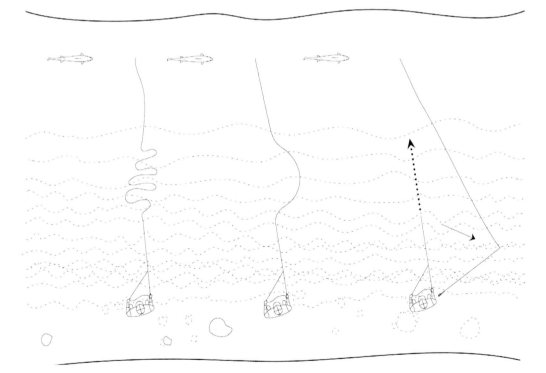

The caster is standing on the edge of fast water and the fish is in slow current. The casts from left to right use an S-mend, a curved mend, and a reach mend.

In this example, you're standing in fast water trying to cast to a fish holding in a slow deep run on the other side of a stream. You're trying to catch this fish on a dry fly with a dead drift. The problem is that the nearer fast water will drag the fly. One solution is to cast across and use a reach mend upstream. Follow the fly downstream with the rod tip. After the fast current starts straightening the mend, throw an on-the-water mend upstream too.

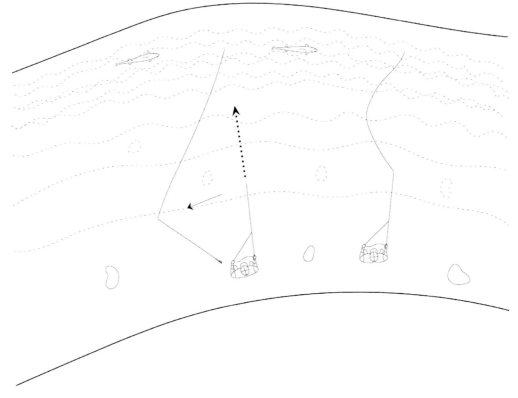

This is the natural problem when entering in slow, shallow water: the main channel where many fish lie is usually running much faster. The presentations from left to right are the reach mend and the curved mend.

SLOW TO FAST CURRENT

You're standing in slow water and you want to cast a nymph for a dead drift into a fast deep current adjacent. The problem is the rear part of the line will not be able to keep up with the rest of the line and will cause an early swing and drag on the fly. The way to avoid this is to make a cast across with a curved mend downstream over the seam between the slow and fast water. As soon as it lands lift the rod tip to keep as much line as possible off the slow water and follow the fly downstream with it.

POCKET WATER BOULDER RUN

Many anglers are hesitant to fish these places because they have many changes in current speed. Many anglers also prefer longer, more graceful presentations. Usually, you will not be able to spot fish here

Boulders create hydraulic cushions and seams as current tries to flow around them. These areas are not hard to read, but you must get a natural drift despite these differences in speed.

unless they feed. Therefore, you should choose the different currents and structures; ahead of the boulder, in each seams of the currents around them, where the currents blend together, and in the deep slick directly behind the boulder. Because the current stalls in front and there is often a deep gouge, big fish will hold there to feed. The front is often a prime lie. I've observed big fish will change their lie around a boulder throughout the day, depending upon the sun and any hatch activity. The hardest location to get a good drift is the cushion behind the boulder because of the current speed change on either side. It might also have a dead spot or circular current. The best casting angle is upstream so you will be casting in the same current as your target fish. Try to let dry flies land before the line so you can hopefully get couple seconds of drag-free drift before the currents pull the line. The best direction to cast and wade would be upstream to prevent detection and let nymphs or other sinking flies sink better.

OVERHANGING COVER OR DOCK

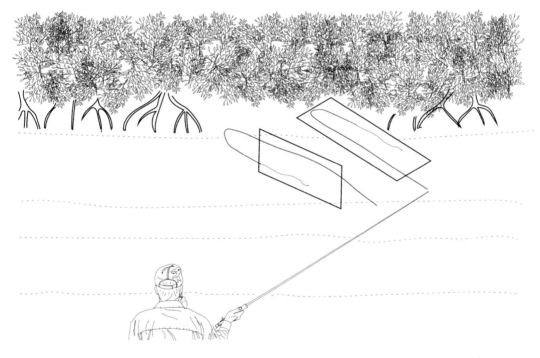

The best way to get under overhanging cover is with a horizontal loop made with a side cast or a pendulum side-cast combo. That way, the loop is flat but the fly is on the bottom and less likely to snag.

I encounter overhanging cover in freshwater streams, estuaries, and saltwater islands. Fish use this cover to seek shade, hunt or ambush prey, and avoid predators. I like using either a low sidearm cast or the pendulum cast to reach underneath. If you're wading, you can decrease the height of your cast by kneeling. The object is not to snag on the delivery and if there is current, cast where there will be enough room for the drift or swing, so you don't snag there, either. When current is running under cover, you can use it to swing a fly underneath and strip it out before it touches a root or dock piling. Of course, if you hook a big fish, all bets are off.

OPEN SPRING CREEK

Spring creeks without a canopy or streams with banks are hard to fish without being seen. This shot shows a sneaky kneeling cast made from the tall grass.

The potential problem in this case is being silhouetted against the sky. Approaching with the sun behind you will not help because your shadow will usually scare fish. Also at low gradient, the current is slow and it's best not to even disturb the water by wading if possible. It is often best to spot a fish and walk around the stream and make a low approach to your chosen casting position. If the stream has high banks, you can choose between wading and not wading. If you wade, you can use the bank as a backdrop and walk low along the stream edge. If the stream does not have banks, you will be wise making your approach on hands and knees. You can cast on your knees or even lying prone or on your side, or you can use a bow-and-arrow cast. This cast is especially good for bank feeders. Practice this on your lawn. The challenge in this situation is not to snag tall grass and brush on the backcast. Make high backcasts and aim low in the front. Sometimes the trout are so spooky, you can't approach the bank or show a rod without being detected. If there is a bank without tall vegetation, cast over land to reach the water. As soon as you hook up, you'll raise the tip off the ground and out of trouble.

BRUSHY STREAM

Small streams usually hold wild, spooky fish. One of the allures of this type of fishing is seeing the color intensity and patterns of these small wild or native fish. Hopefully, you will also not see many anglers. A canopy, banks, and limited backcast room present casting challenges on this kind of water. Because of a short line of sight, fish tend to spot the angler and hide. You can use a roll cast when you can't make a backcast. A bow-and-arrow cast is useful when there is inadequate room for an overhead or roll cast. You can also use any clearance in the shoreline cover for false casts. You can make a Galway cast to place one forward cast through an opening, then make the delivery on the next one. You can also use a Belgian cast to backcast through a hole in the cover, then change directions and cast at your target. Personally, I like to wade quietly upstream so I'm approaching the fish from behind and use the opening above the water, when available, for casting. I limit the amount of wading I do because of the risk of damaging macro invertebrates and vegetation. One way is to walk on any existing trails between spots.

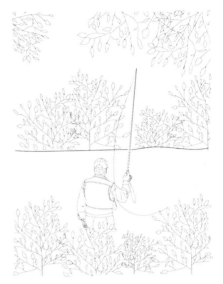

Brushy streams usually have limited space for a backcast. My default cast shown here is a simple roll cast but there are other options depending on the jam you're in.

FIELD TIP

On brushy streams without the room to dry your fly with false casts, bring Shimakatsu drying powder, or amadou to dry it in hand.

BOULDER OBSTRUCTION BETWEEN YOU AND FISH

If you spot a fish rising in a slick on the other side of a boulder, the fast current around the boulder may ruin the drift of your dry fly. To prevent this, cast over the boulder and make a curved mend upstream close to the fly. Let the line land on the boulder. Hold your rod tip up, so the line on your side of the boulder is off the water. The elevation of the boulder will keep line off the fast water immediately alongside it. When you lift the rod, the line will come tight to the fish and the line will lift off the boulder.

The problem shown here is a fish on the other side of a boulder when it is better not to wade for an upstream or downstream presentation.

WIND ON THE FLATS

Even though the wind might be howling, gamefish still feed on the flats. As a matter of fact, the shallows cut big waves down to a light chop and there will be calm water in the lee of islands but plenty of wind. Sometimes when there is some chop, it is the only time you can get close to permit feeding on the flats. The best way to combat strong wind is to use the Barnegat Bay casting with the forward cast

If you get canceled out of a flats trip because of wind but can still wade, find fish on the lee of islands in calm water. You always safely present downwind with your backcast.

into the wind and make a backcast delivery. In most people, the forward cast has more power, so it helps make a good cast. Downwind is a breeze.

CASTING TO GULPERS

There are some great stillwater mayfly hatches and the fish are big and often feed in pods. In the West, mainly the Calibaetis and Grey Drake (Siphlonurus) and in the Midwest and East, the Hexagenias and Grey Drakes (Siphlonurus) are targeted. Caddis, tricos, and midges can also be important stillwater insects. In windy conditions, trout feed into the wind, but when it's calm, they usually cruise around, even in a circle. Many species follow structure such as weeds, breaks, and humps. Since trout cruise to feed in stillwaters and establish a timing pattern between rises, the goal is to watch the course of the fish and anticipate where the fish will rise, so you can lead the fish successfully. If you lead it too far, you stand a chance the fish will rise before it reaches your fly, or miss seeing it if it changes course. If you don't lead it enough, it will spook or pass your fly and rise to a natural on schedule. When you're in a tube or in a boat waiting for fish to rise to one of these hatches or spinnerfalls, you can be ready by keeping your floating line extended on the water in the expected direction until you see your fish. Then pick up the fly, make a backcast, and present it. This will prevent spooking the fish, since there is no false cast over it.

This is Lake Hebgan, Montana, famous for its gulper fishing. You have to be patient and lead the fish properly so that accuracy meets opportunity.

You'll have to practice special presentation casts to master them and you might forget unless you brush up from time to time. Whenever you expend your resources to try new fishing species or destinations, prepare and practice well beforehand.

CHAPTER 6

MAXIMIZING CASTING DISTANCE

In the Northeast where I live, many fly anglers have been resistant to my offers to help them learn to cast longer distances. They contend they don't need any help since their trout casts average thirty feet, or they don't need to cast far because they can almost step on stripers feeding in the trough of the surf. I think many anglers are resistant to help because of the fear of being judged and compared to others. The truth is, no matter what type of fly fishing anglers do, other than in small streams, they can benefit from the ability to cast greater distances. In practice, the same high line speed needed for distance is also required to counter the effects of wind. So maybe a particular angler doesn't need to learn how to cast 100 feet on a still day with a 10-weight, but might need to learn how to cast sixty feet into a strong wind. Or another angler might need to cast thirty feet into a wind with a 4-weight. Although I like fishing alone whenever I can, I see anglers sitting it out when the wind seems too much for them. I believe they too could be enjoying successful fishing.

Many anglers who have not taken the time to improve their distance casting don't know the gains it can provide. Keeping the fly further away from the sound and sight of a boat can mean the difference between a hooked and a scared fish. Being a little farther away also prevents fish from seeing you and your rod while casting. A long cast provides a longer swing in current, or a longer retrieve before the fly reaches the boat. This can result in more bites from species that often follow before striking. If you're wading, anchored, or staked up and don't have time to wade or move the boat closer to a fish, cast farther. When presenting flies to easily frightened wild trout in rivers, you will have fewer close shots than on rivers with stocked fish habituated to humans. Strive to prevail in these challenges.

To make a really long cast with an integrated floating fly line, you must increase the length of the line you carry in the air and increase your line speed. With sinking shooting heads, it's all about speed, good form, and proper overhang. I took up tournament distance casting with shooting heads to help me cast farther for stripers and flats species. I flew out many times and trained with all the distance record holders on the West Coast. We never had a talent hotbed of distance casters in the East to that level. My plan to learn from them worked, and it also helped my distance with floating lines. After learning these distance techniques I returned to flats fishing with one of my first flats guides, Captain Randy Brown. He was so surprised when my cast reached a distant line of tarpon, he said, "Wow, that cast was turbo-charged!" Captain Jim Perry of Middle Torch Key, FL, complimented me on one trip, he said, "Man, you cast a fast line!" All the learning and practice paid off in jumping tarpon and running stripers.

I learned from casting shooting heads, that form is most important for all distance casting and that brute strength isn't the answer to long fishing casts. This concept agrees with the theme of this book. It's about using your head and technique rather than a catapult. In the words of George Dawson, *Fly Casting for Salmon, Fishing with the Fly: Sketches by Lovers of the Art*, Edited by Charles F. Orvis (1883), "If you have a giant's strength, you mustn't use it like a giant. If you do you will never make a long or graceful cast with either trout or salmon rod." In the quest to achieve good distance, you might begin to learn and practice with a careful stroke. When you've got the mechanics down and start casting harder, you will experiment using your maximum effort and find the point of diminishing returns. You'll realize that all-out might ruins form. My friend, ACA and ICSF distance champion, Henry Mittel describes the effort in a cast as: under, normal, maximum, and excessive. The role that strength plays in casting has been misunderstood and I hope to clarify it.

You should take your physical ability into consideration when using heavy tackle and attempting long distances. An instructor or coach should also take your physique into consideration when setting goals for you and recommending tackle. A stronger person can cast much stiffer rods if required and use a shorter stroke than a person with less strength and speed. Long stroke length decreases severity of angle between the rod tip and the rod leg. This reduces the difficulty in accelerating the line. This is why someone with less strength usually uses a longer stroke than a stronger caster. A person with less strength may be able to reach high line speeds with a longer stroke, a rod with a softer action, and achieve comparable distances. We all have our best physical prime in our twenties, but it takes time to develop skill. I've seen remarkable casting by anglers and competitors over fifty. Typically, fifty is when the casting distance scores start to decline in ACA competition. This is due to the decline in muscle mass starting at around age twenty-eight. Casters can extend their peak through exercise and diet. Let's first address body types and how that relates to casting styles and ability.

Let's first address physical characteristics and how that relates to casting styles and ability. The three most determining factors of body build are height, amount of muscle, and the type of muscle fiber. Height can increase distance casting because it increases the potential length of motion of the caster's body and limbs. The amount of muscle mass and type of muscle fiber can affect a caster's rod control and line speed. According to "Muscle, Genes and Athletic Performance" (Andersen, JL; Schjerling, P; Saltin, B., *Scientific American*, 9/2000), there are two major types of muscle fiber: Type I, called slow-twitch muscle fiber, and type II, which has two variations. The first is Type IIa, a combination of fast- and slow-twitch muscle, and Type IIb, which is just fast twitch. Slow is good for endurance and fast is good for explosive speed. A person can have a combination of these types in different parts of the body and in varying amounts. The muscle composition in your body is mainly inherent but can be changed to a certain extent through exercise and diet.

The best competitive distance casters in the world like Steve Rajeff and Henry Mittel are above average in height. Steve is about six feet tall and has a heavy skeletal build with large muscle mass. I know he used to weight train a lot. He has some of the largest hands I've ever seen. Steve uses a compact stroke for distance but explodes on the delivery! Henry is about 6 foot two and thinner in build than Steve, but has great speed enhanced by lots of resistance training. Henry uses more trunk muscles to gain his speed. Height and long arms assist the skills of these casters. Despite these examples, I know many shorter, lighter competitors and anglers with fast twitch muscle who have good hand speed and coordination and can cast very far.

Steve Rajeff's younger brother Tim, who has a less massive frame than Steve's, casts with a longer distance stroke to "build-up speed." Tim is, however, still the only one to cast a perfect 300 Fly Accuracy Combination score at the ACA National Casting Championships, which means he cast all three of our accuracy fly events and didn't miss once! Split-cane rod builder and tournament caster Per Brandin said, "Tim Rajeff is a better natural caster than his brother Steve." Per remembers Tim hitting the bell in the casting pool with a plug every time while riding a skateboard! Tim was probably the first to relate this golf advice from Harvey Pennic to new casters, "Find the best [caster] in the world and copy their style but only do so if you are built like them." Once you are comfortable with your style of casting, work on efficiency. Tight loops, plus high line speed, plus trajectory and direction equals distance.

CONDITIONS AND WIND: TRAJECTORY AND CASTING DIRECTION

Steve Rajeff has told me and other disciples, you want a climbing loop to maximize distance. Ideally, you want to aim the trajectory so the loop and leader unroll and lose momentum just before landing. If you aim so high that the leader straightens and falls many feet straight down before landing, you've aimed too high and probably lost a few feet of casting distance. If you aim too low, you will shorten distance potential. We see this plainly when we take turns pegging the landing of the fly and measuring casts at the National Championships. When throwing the discus or javelin, the athlete faces the same challenge. In these throwing sports, this trajectory is called the angle of attack. Paul Arden says he aims at real or imaginary "sky" targets for backcasts and long delivery casts. For maximum distance, the trajectory should include the relative height of the caster and the water. For example, trajectory should be lower when deep wading versus standing on a bow platform or jetty.

We even have to factor gravity vs. favorable air and wind conditions in the trajectory of our casts. All other variables being equal, casting trajectory should also vary with line density, fly weight, and resistance. High-density sinking lines are less air resistant than floating lines and will need a higher trajectory to make a longer flight than a more resistant line of the same weight. Casting with a big, air-resistant fly requires a lower trajectory. Some things you can't change, like the weather, other things like casting angle and trajectory, you can.

The environmental conditions where we cast have a great influence on the flight of the line, especially in respect to distance. The assistance of wind behind a cast can add dozens of feet to our distance. Wind against our casts can cause them to fail completely. Use wind to your advantage for safety, distance, and energy conservation. Whenever you can wade or position a boat to present your fly downwind, it's to your advantage. It will be harder to back-cast into the wind but a last false cast isn't as far as a forward cast shot into the distance. The next-best angle is quartering with the wind on the side of your line hand. It will keep the fly away from you and still help sail your line and fly in your casting direction.

Casting downwind reduces air resistance in frontal areas because of decreased relative speed, and the wind pulls and pushes the cast downwind. The backside of a loop has a concave surface like a sail. When a caster wants to set a distance record, the two most-desired ACA Nationals host clubs are Long Beach, California, and Toronto, Canada, sitting above Lake Ontario. These bodies of water are weather-making wind generators and can produce humidity. A headwind will have an effect on timing forward casts, because loops will stay aloft longer downwind on the backcast, due to lift and drag. But they open faster.

Altitude, barometric pressure, air temperature, and humidity all affect air density. The lower the air density, the less air resistance, or drag. This drag slows the flight of a cast and lets gravity work more quickly to pull your cast earthward. There is an opposite relationship between lift and drag in relation to increases and decreases in air density. Increases in air density increase lift, which helps the flight of your line. Conversely, the higher the air density is, the higher the drag and air resistance on the flight of a cast. Drag seems to have more effect on distance than lift does. From my experience, all things being equal, casting in low air density with low drag, is best for distance casting. An example would be casting at high altitude with high humidity.

The effect of decreased drag due to decreased barometric pressure at increased altitude has been proven at the International Sportmen's Expositions, Best of the West 5-weight competitions in the Rocky Mountains, and in California near sea level. The casting distance of the same competitors was greater at high altitude. Humidity decreases air drag too. When humidity increases, the density of the air decreases and its resistance against a moving object decreases. This observation concerning humidity may seem contrary to what you'd expect. In explaining the characteristics of humidity, sport enthusiast and physicist Peter Brancazio states:

> You may find this surprising, since the air often feels 'heavy' on humid days but this feeling arises from body physiology (perspiration evaporates more slowly when the air is damp) and not from the actual density of the air. In damp air, oxygen and nitrogen molecules are replaced by lighterweight water molecules. Thus damp air weighs less than dry air at the same temperature and pressure. Changes in air density due to humidity are normally not very large . . . for example at 86° Fahrenheit and 80 percent humidity the air is about 1 percent less dense than dry air

at the same temperature and pressure. Nevertheless, moving objects are subject to less drag at higher humidity.

So high altitude and high humidity would be ideal, but climatologically they are not usually concurrent. So, this will help reconcile your casting performance in different parts of the country and under different weather conditions.

USING THE BODY

Mel Krieger was the first casting coach I heard talk about the path of energy and biomechanics in distance casting. In his video, *The Essence of Flycasting II* (2003), he says, "It's kind of an uncoiling, it starts right at the feet and just works up; through the knees, hips, shoulders, elbow, hand, the rod tip." If you can use body movement to assist casting without spooking your quarry, it will help you make longer casts. Body movement can increase casting distance in four ways; increase line tension in the cast, help get the casting arm and rod moving in the direction of their acceleration, increase translation, and it can also add to rod load. The timing, amount, and direction of the body movement will affect how it accomplishes each of these elements.

Your stance is the foundation for a long cast. Extending your base increases stability to effectively transfer your body weight in the direction of your casts. Most of us put the line hand side foot forward, which creates a body block to push against and enables the most travel, but casters in the past, like Marvin Hedge, put their opposite foot forward. This prevents tracking error by limiting body rotation with a different type of body block. To start a distance cast, the front knee should be bent and your weight on the back foot. Turn the back foot outward so you can push forward on the delivery with the long edge of the foot.

Hip and waist rotation are on a vertical axis and increase the length of movement in the direction of the cast and the time over which we accelerate. The same thing is true for shoulder rotation which helps increase delivery stroke length, while helping maintain good tracking. In *Sport Mechanics for Coaches*, 3rd Edition, (2010), Dr. Brendan Burkett explains three reasons to rotate the hips when throwing a baseball or javelin and I believe it also applies to a distance cast. First, it accelerates the body's mass in the direction of our throw. Second, hip rotation is a link in the "sequential acceleration of the athlete's body segments." This " . . . simulates swinging a handle ahead of the whip so the tip of the whip will crack." Third, " . . . the rotation of the hips stretches the muscles of the abdomen and chest so they

Hip rotation helps accelerate the cast by increasing the total stroke and helping move the upper body in the direction of the cast.

pull the shoulders and throwing arm in slingshot fashion toward the direction of throw."

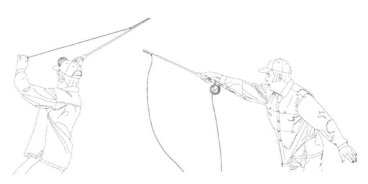

Shoulder rotation also helps accelerate the cast by increasing the total stroke and helping move the casting arm in the casting direction.

The distance casting sequence should start by bending the knees slightly and slightly bending backward during the backcast and forward during the forward cast, while transferring the body weight fore and aft in combination with the rotational torso movements. On the final presenting cast, the caster should set up by progressively bending the knees, arch the torso and transfer weight backward until the caster feels or sees the backcast timing cues to initiate the delivery. The body should move a millisecond before the forward stroke. The caster directs the forward body movement and extension in the direction of the cast, forward and upward. This torso and knee flexion in the direction of the cast can have a profound effect on rod loading, because it adds to rod rotation.

LOOP SHAPE AND TURNOVER FOR DISTANCE

A wedge-shaped, or "chiseled" loop will be less air-resistant than one with a round shape. I covered many of the techniques for making an efficient loop previously, but for distance there are a few special techniques for maintaining a pointed loop while producing maximum line speed. To increase your casting distance, you have to maintain sound casting mechanics. As you push the envelope, errors can

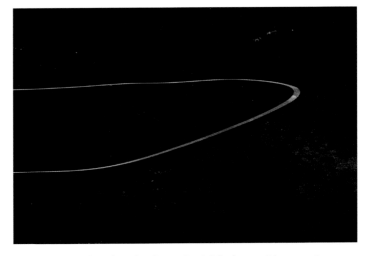

A wedge-shaped loop has the sharpest point for less resistance and an inclined rod leg I think creates lift.

occur. Poor tracking is one major error and it can be a big distance robber.

Line speed, the line design, and the amount of overhang determine the rate of loop turnover. Overhang is the length of running or shooting line extended from the tip ring to the head while casting. When a tight loop is unrolling, it is energized and aerodynamic. The longer unrolling is delayed and forward momentum continued, the farther the cast will go. Increased head length increases cast length in two ways. It delays loop opening and the additional carried line adds directly to the cast length. Let's say you can shoot sixty feet of running line regardless of head length and it will turn over completely. Using a ten-foot longer head will directly add ten feet to the cast. A longer front taper delays opening too, but if it's too long, it might not open at all. If a line is designed without one, the turnover is fast and abrupt. So, for increased distance, select lines or heads with the longest belly you can carry in the air and reasonable front taper that will turn over.

Overhang affects the cast in two ways. First, the length of overhang adds to the total length of line you are carrying and to total casting distance. Secondly, overhang delays turnover. There is a point of diminishing returns when increasing the overhang. If the overhang is too long, the line gets wavy, unstable, and the loop can collapse. Since wind drag supports the line and helps maintain tension, use a short overhang in low wind conditions and increase its length in higher wind, until you find the sweet spot.

STROKE MECHANICS FOR DISTANCE

To increase your delivery speed for more distance, you must use the body properly and make the appropriate length stroke and haul for your potential. Depending upon your strength and speed as described in the previous sections, you will either be more productive using a long or a short style of casting stroke. You may have confidence in one of several different grip styles for making distance casts. Whichever style you use, you must accelerate the cast smoothly. If you use the Western style of casting, you will want to lead with the elbow and have approximately two 90 degree joint angles before making a long cast. The first is at the shoulder; the second is at the elbow. This is the same relation as the position before making a baseball pitch.

The greater the length of the compound movements in the stroke, the more chances for tracking errors. Integrated fly lines are like a kite with a tail and have some inherent stability and self-correct flight defects caused by some tracking errors. Shooting heads are not as forgiving. They have a tendency to pile if the acceleration isn't smooth and the tracking isn't true. So if you have a long stroke, there will need to be some compensatory movement to keep the hand moving in one plane from front to back. Since the longest stroke is the full extension of one's forward delivery, the caster should check it for proper tracking. Many of us have a tendency to rotate at the waist for extension and cross our casting arm over before the end of the stroke, instead of forward toward the target. It shouldn't look like the follow-through of a baseball pitcher. The best way to keep the move straight is to turn at the waist and open the shoulder and reach in the direction of the target.

For the sake of simplicity, the length of a casting stroke should be only as long as required to cast the length of line used. So, when false casting before a distance presentation, the false cast stroke should be relative to the length of the cast and therefore not your longest. To make the final cast, there should be changes to body and arm position to input the most practical amount of acceleration to the line in the proper direction. The object is to accelerate the rod so that the resulting bend will produce a straight rod-tip path. This will be produced mainly by the stroke; the path of the casting hand. The arm and hand position before making the stroke determine which muscles are involved and are critical for maximizing the centripetal force on the rod. This is a force that pulls or pushes an object toward the axis of rotation in order to make it follow a curved or circular pathway. They are also critical for making the longer stroke.

A distance cast requires increased stroke arc, which includes any translation needed to make the rod tip follow a straight path. It's a given that the hand will travel as far forward as possible on the delivery. There are also two ways to start the stroke further rearward to increase the stroke arc; by bringing the rod hand further back on the last backcast, or by drifting.

Drifting is a rearward repositioning of the rod hand after the backcast stop to lengthen the stroke of the forward delivery cast. This movement should be about three

In this illustration of drift, the hand moves a few inches rearward during the pause.

inches or you will be adding slack. Instead of a rearward move and an increase in stroke length, you can rotate the wrist backward and open the rod arc. Some call this rotational drift. Jason Borger calls it layback in his book, *Nature of Fly Casting* (2001).

Some casters also include some upward repositioning of the casting hand. This raises the straightening rod leg of the backcast and sets up the casting hand for additional downward rotation on the forward cast. Another repositioning move is called drag. Drag is intentional forward rod movement to increase tension and remove slack. Drag doesn't load the rod. Total stroke length and arc must be taken into consideration when adding drag or tailing can result. With the body and casting arm cocked in a manner of the caster's choosing, the line straightened but not falling, the caster starts the forward cast.

The forward delivery on a long distance cast should start with slightly increased grip pressure during smooth acceleration of the rod with a long simultaneous haul. The muscles of the body will be contracted and effort should be made to stabilize the rod in hand to track straight ahead. As rod loading is sensed by the wrist, it should open to add the final rotation. Varying the rate of wrist rotation can be used to minimize slack during the cast and will be one determinant of the rod bend. As the stroke progresses, weight transfer and forward extension of all body segments should be accumulative. A rod-stopping sequence should begin with the straightening of the arm and increased grip pressure again and the rapid turnover of the wrist. This should produce rod rotation and high line speed. The line hand making the haul should end up near mid-thigh and release the line into the cast as the rod straightens. As the speed of the line overtakes the speed of the rod tip, the loop is being formed. As the wrist of the rod hand passes a straight position, as does the rod, and the arm should thrust the rod upward. This movement is called thrusting and helps maintain a straight rod-tip path and tighten the rod leg of the loop. After the thrust, grip pressure should be minimized, allowing the rod to absorb its vibration instead of the hand increasing the amplitude and imparting it to the line.

When we false cast or make short to medium length casts, we use our muscles to contract and stop the rod to make a tight loop. When we make a long delivery cast, we don't limit the forward stroke with a stop in that manner. The caster stops the rod at the end of cast when he "runs out of arm" as he rotates the wrist, then snaps the elbow straight. Stopping the rod doesn't cause a loop to form.

This photo shows the end position of the full arm extension on a distance cast called Thrust.

Stopping the rod when the rod tip is close to its straight-line path, makes a tight loop, as just described. Stopping lower or later increases the size of the loop. What the caster does after the loop is formed also has an influence on keeping the loop tight and aerodynamic. Bruce Richards shared in an email to Gordy Hill's Master Study Group:

> Depending on the caster's intentions though, the rod can also stop completely. Or even stop, then rotate a bit in the other direction. Those stops make the tightest loops as they keep the bottom leg the highest, but they also usually have significant 'bumps' in the bottom leg as they accentuate rod counterflex/ rebound rather than temper it.

HAULS AND SHOOTING LINE FOR DISTANCE

Nothing can add more line speed more than good hauling. The most important hauling factors are timing, length, and speed. For a maximum length cast, the hauling hand holding the running line should be as close to the stripping guide as practical to maximize the length of the haul. The release of the line should be made where the path of the haul passes the thigh and the hand should follow through unless the line hand fingers are used as a line guide. The line flows through an O shape made with the index and thumb can prevent a tangle and be used to stop a cast on a target. Using it as a guide creates some resistance and lessens distance.

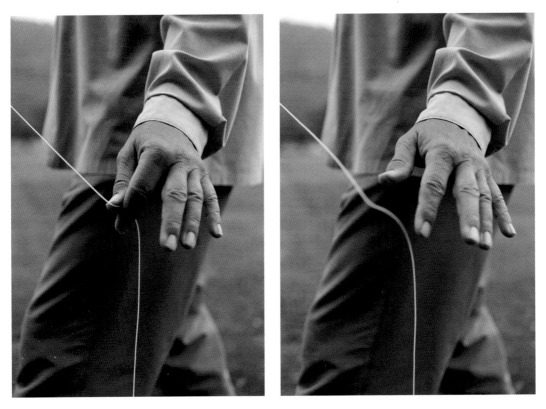

I thought I'd show the hand position for the longest haul release because it happens so fast.

GENERAL DISTANCE TRAINING

If you want to perform some exercises to increase your stroke and hauling speed, I can share a few. Here's one Chris Korich taught me at the 2004 Northwestern Tournament in San Francisco. You can do this drill even if you don't have room for a backcast. Perform the longest roll casts permitted so you still have the rear taper in the tip guide. Make sure your casting hand forearm is vertical or even angled slightly back. This arm position will include and condition your deltoid muscles. Do this for forty minutes every session as often as your schedule can accommodate. Chris reassured me of the resistance this drill offers, "Remember, your rod and reel might not weigh five pounds plus, but your arm surely does." You can do this drill on water or make a roll cast tool for the lawn as did Craig Buckbee, IFFF MCI. Craig's catches the line when you cast

This tool designed by NYS Guide and IFFF MCI, Craig Buckbee, helps hold and release the line to simulate and practice roll casts on land.

into the V of the tool and holds the line at the nail knot as you raise your rod tip, then releases the line on the forward cast.

Another way to train to increase distance is progressive distance training on the grass. Pick a spot where you can consistently cast in the same wind direction each time. You can set up in two different directions. First, you cast with the wind 90 degrees to your casting direction and on your line hand side and the drill will not favor either your backcast or your forward cast and you can train equally. Second, you can cast downwind, which will help you measure tracking accurately with no side wind and its effects. The wind at your back will help you develop a strong backcast and will also let you realize good loop turnover on the forward cast. To start, warm up and then cast as far as possible without compromising your form. Measure the cast and note the wind speed. End the session and repeat another day. Each session, try to incrementally increase your distance until you run out of line. If you're casting downwind, take variances in wind speed into account. You can cast around 30 percent farther in a good wind than in calm.

CASTING 10–14-WEIGHT FLY OUTFITS AND HEAVY FLIES

Fly fishing with heavy one-handed outfits requires the most physically demanding cast in our sport. The number of casts you make per day, the cast length, fly weight, and the wind speed will determine the physical requirements. The demands become greater and the rods stiffer and heavier as you increase line weight, fly size, and weight. Therefore, it pays to learn efficient technique and also prepare your body in advance if you don't participate in activities or train in a way that get you ready.

An angler mainly uses these rods from boats in saltwater. The major techniques are blind casting, bait-and-switch (see Presentation) and sight fishing. I would include structure fishing within blind casting if no feeding fish are visible at the surface. The structure could be shore, exposed reef, or submerged structure only indicated by mapping or sonar. I would also include casting to blitzing schools of fish in sight casting. In some cases you only need to make short casts, in other cases, the object is to cast as far as possible.

Blind casting requires the most numbers of casts per trip and usually

I've shown stiff 12- and 14-weight outfits to emphasize how casting them well will take some preparation. They really aren't so hard to cast after becoming accustomed to them.

requires your maximum casting distance. An example would be blind casting in a muddy basin for tarpon with a 12-weight. In a day of bait and switch fishing for billfish, you might make a few casts or maybe fifty. It won't tire you as much as playing a few billfish. When you're sight fishing on the flats for permit, giant trevaly, sharks, or tarpon, the number of casts is few and fighting these fish will be far more fatiguing than casting to them. The same is true if you're cruising the Gulfstream casting for dolphin along Sargasso weed or flotsam. In the western Atlantic, the most common schooling gamefish are striped bass, bluefish, little tunny, tuna, redfish, and jack crevalle. Fishing for them when they're surface feeding usually requires long casts so the boat will not put them down. If the fishing is good, you might be required to make a couple hundred casts in a full day! On the other hand, if you're live-chumming with the engines off, you won't need to cast far, or often.

I've already covered the saltwater quick cast and how to cast heavy lines and flies in the chapter on Presentation. In addition to those techniques, I use some others exclusively when using heavy tackle. An angler mostly uses floating lines for sight fishing on the flats. When fly fishing in the deeper inshore and offshore locations, sinking heads or full sinking line are best. Not only do they sink deeper but their thinner diameter makes them less wind resistant and therefore, easier to cast. For some species and circumstances you'll need to throw a large wind-resistant fly. One tip before you fish one is to attach it to your line and sink it to saturate it in water. Wetting it will streamline it and give it more casting weight. If your first cast is an important one, this tip will also help it sink to its intended depth, instead of sitting on the surface until it sinks.

The most difficult part of casting heavy tackle is getting the fly safely out of the water, and moving fast enough to load the rod with little line out. If I strip a fly all the way in, I'll combine a roll cast with shooting to extend the line and load the rod. It starts by holding the rod to the side, close to the water, and slowly enlarging the little

Wind-resistant flies like this shark fly take a heavy outfit to deliver them in wind.

oval with the rod tip with accelerating speed, shooting line on each pick-up and lay-down. Start raising the rod tip as the oval enlarges and when you've got about twenty feet of line out, shoot the fly either backward or forward until it lands on the water and waterload it into the next cast. Once you've done this, you can double haul and shoot a couple of false casts to present your fly.

If you're retrieving a fly when swinging on rips, as I detailed in my 2012 *Fly Fisherman Magazine* article, "Squid in the Rips", heavy current is an added difficulty. When the boat is stemming the tide, the tide will swing your fly until it's straight astern and you have to strip into the beginning of the head in order to start a change-of-direction cast. I've found using a snap-T cast effectively repositions the fly for a pick-up into an overhead cast, regardless of whether I'm delivering with my forward or my back cast.

Blind casting heavy loads with heavy rods for hours on end can cause a blister on the base of the index finger of your casting hand. I've practiced casting heavy outfits months ahead of fishing season to toughen my hands and it doesn't help. Constantly wet hands in saltwater soften calluses which soon detach internally and rip off. Gloves don't even help! To prevent this from occurring, don't squeeze the grip so hard and limit the number of casts per day. If a guide wants you to kill time blind casting when there is no tide or real prospects, you can say no thank you. If possible, fish half the day with your dominant hand and the other half with your non-dominant hand. If that doesn't work for you, try a two-handed rod.

The way for healthy muscles and joints to become conditioned for heavy tackle is to start with a lighter outfit than your goal and increase the weight of the whole outfit every two sessions. For most people accustomed to lighter tackle, they will find a point in rod/line weight where they begin to lose distance before special training. So if you're used to light trout gear, you might start practicing with an 8-weight and go up the ladder until you've reached your goal. This is an example of the principle of overloading used in weight training. Always warm up before strenuous activity and train with the approval of your physician. You can also train using tools for strengthening your wrists, like the Digi-Flex or Powerball. A cable machine or resistance bands are great tools to overload your muscles to practice the stroke or the haul.

After casting with a yarn fly, practice with a hookless practice fly that is the same size and weight as the fly you'll be using. I usually make one by sacrificing a chewed-up fly and cut the hook off at the bend. Start your casts slowly and build speed. The goal will be maximum line speed and tight loops. This will require using your body, making very long forward strokes, positive rod stops, and long hauls.

Practice your saltwater quick casts for boat or wading. When you're comfortable with your outfits, try using the wind like a sailor. Get used to feeling the wind direction with your ears. Practice your wind casts from all directions. Cast at targets at all distances if you're training for sight fishing. The mechanics or form used to make faster, longer, more accurate casts in any weather condition can be learned, controlled, and practiced. It will just take your desire, time, and sometimes some help.

CHAPTER 7

TACKLE

The physical weight of rods and reels and their balance is an individual and controversial issue. The angle at which you hold your rod and the distance you hold it away from your body and length of time, will determine how much leverage the rod has on your body. Most modern fly fishermen agree light rods and reels are better. Even Vince Marinaro advocated light outfits over forty years ago and in his book *In the Ring of the Rise* (2001) he states why R.C. Leonard proved his point in 1889 by smashing all distance records by being first to compete without a reel attached to his fly rod: "That the caster must move the useless weight below the hand as well as the useful weight above the hand; that the removal of dead weight below the hand helped to overcome inertia more quickly, increasing the tip speed, thus imparting a greater velocity to the projectile or fly line."

Light outfits can be cast with more speed and less fatigue. The less a rod and reel combination weighs, the quicker you can accelerate and decelerate it with the casting hand. Let's say we have two 5-weight rod outfits with identical line and action but one rod weighs three ounces, or a third more than the other. If you can decelerate the lighter rod butt and lighter rod tip in less distance, you will cast tighter loops. As a bonus, less mass out at the end of your rod helps protect a light tippet when you quickly lift it in response to a take. Holding lighter outfits for extended periods takes less effort too.

RODS

Out of all their tackle, anglers have the most love for their rods. We love the feel of their cork handles, the bend of their action, and the loops they can throw. Experienced anglers start hoarding rods they like and some run out of storage room in their caves. Many anglers who learned to cast in the era of bamboo and fiberglass have opposite concerns about rod feel and performance than advocates of current technology. At a recent nostalgic fly fishing show I saw bamboo rod builders giving out magnetic signs saying, "Say No to Plastic!" These gentlemen say they want to feel and see the bend caused by the weight of the rod during the cast so they can keep better timing. They also want to feel a rod bend more than most graphite designs allow. At least two rod manufacturers heard this plea and produced models with slower actions recently than they have made in years.

Most anglers who learned to cast and fly fish in the era of graphite think of rods as tools and compare models and brands for performance and anticipate advances in equipment as much as they do new computers or smartphones. We've learned to accept obsolescence and constantly raising the bar. I just hope that anglers take the time to understand how rods work and experiment a little instead of choosing a rod based on hype. Now I'm going to analyze the function and variations of rod action.

ROD ACTION

When choosing a rod of a given task, you first have to consider action. There are rods that are good all around rods and others that are designed to do one thing superbly. I try to understand the requirements and when practical, bring the best rod for a fishing situation. Action describes the bending characteristics of a rod or blank. The "speed" of a rod's action, "slow" vs. "fast," is where it bends under strain. Rod makers use a tool called a deflection board, or tester, to measure the curve of the action when a test weight is hung from its tip and the rod butt is in a holder at a fixed angle. A "slow" action rod bends throughout its length almost equally and a "fast" action rod bends more toward the tip. How much the rod bends at a given point indicates its stiffness. A "soft" rod bends more overall than the majority of rods of the same line weight. A "stiff" rod is one that bends less than the majority of rods in the same line weight. These terms describe the static properties of rod action.

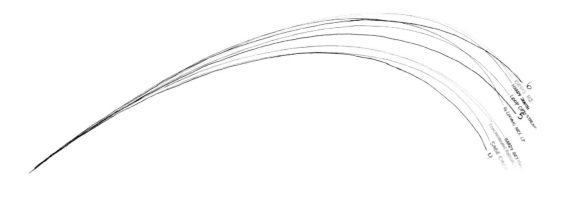

This is the "Top Rods" deflection board Yellowstone Angler in Livingston, MT, made to record and compare rod actions in their 2013 5-wt Shootout. Photo and drawing courtesy Yellowstone Angler

The dynamic properties of rod action are how it loads and unloads when cast. The action of the rod determines potential line speed, how tight a loop it will cast, and how easily it can manipulate line and protect light tippets. The total weight and weight distribution for a given length rod will affect how fast the caster can accelerate or decelerate the rod, and the rate the rod unloads. The weight characteristics also affect how much and how fast the rod counterflexes and how fast it rebounds. This bend in counterflex will pull down and open the loop. The slower the rod rebounds, the more negative its affect on the loop. So, excessive softness and rod weight are detrimental to a tight loop and subsequently, line speed and distance potential. On the other hand, it is easier to manipulate line for slack line presentations, curves, and mends with a softer rod. The counterflex that opens loops, aids when making these casts.

The stiffer a rod is, to the point of diminishing returns, the more potential it has for high line speed. A stiff, light rod will unload with greater speed than a soft, light one. It is easier to haul effectively with a stiffer action rod than a softer one too. There is less angle between the guides due to lesser bend, thus less friction. But, if a rod is so stiff a caster is unable to load, or bend the rod sufficiently in a cast, it has little potential to cast a tight loop and cast far. You need the rotation and speed of the straightening rod for high line speed. A real example of the effects of proper versus excessive fly rod stiffness is in a Norwegian study; "*eight rods—eight casters: test of five line rods*" online at Sexyloops.com, a progressive fly fishing website operated by Paul Arden. It's an indoor distance test using athletic and experienced casters. The results showed several commercial 5-weight rods were too stiff and softer rods in the selection beat them in distance results! On the extreme, you can cast a tight loop with a very soft rod but line speed is limited. This will reduce casting distance. As you create more and more speed with the soft rod, the rod tip will not travel in a straight enough line for tight loops (see Chapter 2).

The action and weight characteristics in a rod are determined by the design, materials, and components used to build it. As I mentioned earlier, weight can also affect action. These attributes determine suitability for distance, presentation, fighting ability, and reliability. If the rod is light and a pleasure to cast, you'll also enjoy it longer.

ROD MATERIALS & CONSTRUCTION

I first learned to fish with tubular metal and glass plug rods, then glass fly rods, etc. I reveled with each reduction in weight and improvement in rod action. One such improvement was by Jim Green of Fenwick who invented the first tip-over-butt ferrule called the Feralite, patented in 1965. Compared to the heavier and rigid metal ferrules preceding it, this helped the action and reliability of composite rods. Carbon fiber, commonly known as graphite, was the biggest game changer in terms of weight. I built my first tarpon rod in the '80s from an IM6 Sage blank and watched as IMX and GLX evolved in the blanks manufactured by Gary Loomis. I was so enamored with GLX in the mid '90s, I kept their first product catalogs and had Steve Rajeff autograph them when we did a casting event together in 2010.

Today, fly anglers have the choice of new rods with actions ranging from slow to extra fast and a range of physical weights. You can spend from $100 for beginner rods to $5,000 for custom bamboo. You can get rods and blanks from one to seven pieces. No matter what anyone tells you, the fewer ferrules, or lack of them in a rod, the less loss of action it will suffer and the lighter it will be. Multipiece rods are a convenience or even a necessity in travel and shipping. The variations in design I'm about to describe include the use of different components and the different materials, taper, and variables of the blank.

If you've ever read a book on rod building by an expert like Dale Clemens or Art Scheck, you'll remember being instructed to locate rod guides in relation to the rod spine. Spine is the stiffest longitudinal side of a blank when flexed. The traditional rod building practice has been to locate the guides on the spine for fly and spin rods and opposite for baitcasting rods. This theoretically provides more stiffness for the forward cast. According to Steve Rajeff, Senior Rod Designer at G.Loomis:

As the spine is a moving target, we place guides on fly rods to make for the straightest appearance when sighting down the guides. Spine is created by the blank wall thickness and is not even all around the blank. For most rods, the material wraps needed for action and strength increases from tip to butt, and causes the change of wall thickness. A blank may have three wraps of material to start with at the tip, three to five wraps at middle, and six to ten wraps near the butt. The "spine" may be very different in orientation if you are getting an overall bend, or just loading the top third of rod. The spine actually spirals down the blank, and is why I call it a moving target. We believe the spine is of small consequence in fly rod casting/fishing, and to prove it, concentrate on the feel and stiffness of the fly rod while casting for a minute. Then, rotate the rod in hand by 90 degrees and cast some more. Then, flip it 180 degrees the other way. I bet there is not any noticeable stiffness difference. The only time we are careful to locate the spine is for stand up casting rods, where we expect a severe rod bend, and want the guides to remain in upright position when fighting the fish. We use a ball bearing rotation holding fixture/tool, to locate the spine.

Most of the other major manufacturers do not spine their rods either and simply place the guides on the straightest portion of the rod when viewed horizontally. According to a video on Winston's website, they put their guides on the convex arch of the blank to cause it to straighten with gravity.

Today's materials include bamboo, fiberglass, or graphite composites. Each material has its own inherent strengths and working limitations. The ultimate finished product has varying intended applications and much of a rod's desirability to anglers is subjective. I'm now going to explore these material choices with you.

BAMBOO

I recently read a book by John McDaniel, titled *Fly Fishing the Harriman Ranch* (2012), in which he says his preferred rod, the one he fishes as often as possible, is built of cane by Per Brandin: "The number of fish I *hooked* per hour was higher with cane than with modern graphite rods!" This made me want to understand why he could catch more Henry's Fork bows with these split-cane rods than any other rod, regardless of material. Per is currently one of the best split-cane rod makers and his rods exhibit minimalist elegance and beauty. He is also a past president of the Oakland Casting Club. Since Per and I are ACA casting

This is a four-strip Per Brandin bamboo rod and a detail of his hollow building. Photo courtesy Per Brandin, Split-Cane Rods

friends and live in adjacent states, I asked him if I could spend a day with him to learn about the history, construction, and feel of bamboo in preparation for this book. Per said, "Just from a rod design point of view, what I want to show you are standard, tapered rods, like an eight and a half foot Payne; a different action idea, a parabolic tapered rod from Paul Young in Michigan; an early Gary Howells rod, which is hollow in the butt and solid in tip; my tournament Trout Fly Rod—it kind of embodies all the things we've been talking about. It's almost like casting a graphite rod." We had been talking about lightening a bamboo rod as much as possible by hollow building and creating the best action and feel.

I was able to cast very tight loops with almost all the rods of different actions using a different stroke than I would for today's composites, but some of the older, less-sophisticated designs were quite heavy. Most bamboo rods use metal ferrules that add some weight and affect the action more than sleeve or spigot composite ferrules. The problem with excessive rod weight isn't just caster fatigue.

There is a causal relationship between increasing physical weight of a rod and the slowness of its action, deceleration, and recovery. Today's bamboo designs can be lighter than their predecessors because the new glues are stronger, enabling a builder to save weight by using shorter glue lines in the design. Not only does this require less glue, but you can also save weight by hollowing out the rod more than before. Per also makes four-strip rods with a taped spliced-joint that saves weight and preserves more action. Per told me another interesting fact, a bamboo rod of a given line weight has to be stiffer than a comparable one made of composite because the builder needs to compensate for the greater physical weight of the bamboo rod. I learned a lot from Per that day and I felt a new reverence for him and the breadth of knowledge he has earned from years of study, collaboration, and experience.

I believe bamboo rod lovers appreciate the craftsmanship and nostalgia, the natural and artistic beauty, and the feedback of the rod's action. I don't think John McDaniel catches more big bows because Per's rods are superior in performance to the best graphite rods; I think he uses them because they give him confidence. I believe using them makes him get closer to these spooky trout and enjoy the presentation casts more intensely. John also justifiably speculates that the duller finish on Per's rods don't scare trout as much as a shinier one. Better position, as well as the feeling of the rod's action probably increase his concentration and reduces mistakes. After I successfully fished tiny dry flies at the Ranch this September in calm and very windy conditions with my ultra modern outfits, I visited Per and cast his wonderful 834-2 df HB, the one John McDaniel loves. The rod cast very well. The flame treatment of the bamboo gives it gorgeous honey hues and the finish has a stealthy hand rubbed satin sheen. Despite how much I liked the test drive, I don't subconsciously crave to feel more rod action than I feel with my graphite rods. I also recently got to know cane rod builder Bob Colson and cast an eight-foot 5-weight he built that was surprisingly fast. Despite my new appreciation for split-cane rods and their makers, I will continue fishing my light tubular composite fly rods with confidence and await any improvements in design or materials.

FIBERGLASS

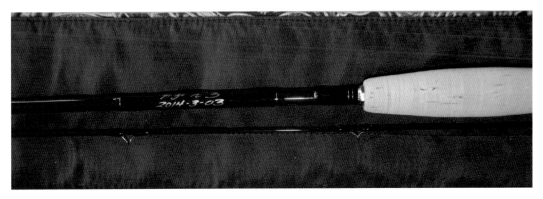

This is probably the most sought-after fiberglass rod made today. It is made by the Tom Morgan Rodsmiths. Photo courtesy Tom Morgan Rodsmiths

Approximately ten major fly rod manufacturers offer fiberglass rods. Some are blending-in some graphite but the emphasis is on slower action and more feedback than graphite for up-close accuracy and ease of casting. Because of the increased weight of glass, the rods I investigated were between six and a maximum of about eight feet in length. Some manufacturers are charging almost as much for their glass rods as for graphite, while others are using a lower price point as an advantage. The number of glass collectors and angler/builders has increased lately too. ACA Hall of Famer Chris Korich, who used to work with Jimmy Green at Fenwick, thinks stiff tip, full flex rods are more efficient than modern, tippy, fast, graphite rod tapers. His stroke is a downward chop with his preferred glass Fenwick HMG rods.

GRAPHITE, BORON & QUARTZ

Steve Rajeff says that when it comes to building effective composite rods, design outweighs materials. In Steve's words:

> Modulus is the measurement of resistance to strain, expressed as a ratio. In the context of fishing rod design, it describes the stiffness of the fiber used to construct the rod. It does not by itself determine rod stiffness, weight or strength. High modulus materials can be used to make soft rods, and conversely, low modulus material can be designed into making stiff rods. Several other important measurements of rod material to consider include fiber strength, elongation, compression rate, resin content percentage and resin toughness, scrim type and weight. The goal of many rod makers is to optimize these variables, achieve the desired action (combined taper and stiffness), high strength at low weight and reasonable cost.

The rods Steve has designed for the ACA distance events optimize high line speed but are only under G.Loomis warranty for tournament casting, since their thin wall construction is not designed to stand up to the strains of fighting fish. Using stiff, light materials also helps the finished rod transmit vibrations back to the angler's hand.

In addition to graphite, other materials have been used to reinforce or stiffen blanks in a way to reduce weight. Back in the 1990s, Redington Fly Fishing had a line of rods called the Nano Titanium Quartz. It was popular and cast well but was not cost effective. In 1998, Winston started using boron in its fly rods and still does as of this writing. I spoke to Winston's chief rod designer Annette McLean recently to ask about their use of boron. Annette confirmed that they use a boron and graphite matrix solely in the butt section of Winston's Boron series of rods. She says, "It is used to take dead weight off the butt of the rod. We can use less material and reduce the diameter of the rod butt with boron, which is stronger than graphite alone and increases power and strength. It's like the turbocharger in the rod." Gatti Fly Fishing in Italy dropped its line of boron/graphite rods, as did Wright and McGill in the US, in favor of all graphite. If you look at George Anderson's Yellowstone Angler Fly Rod Shootouts online, you will see that no rods containing boron are impressively lighter than the ones that beat them in the overall contest.

ROD LENGTH

Rod length is the next big criteria when selecting a rod. Properly designed, additional rod length adds additional line speed and thus additional casting distance for situations like big river and saltwater fishing. According to rod designer Don Phillips in *The Technology of Fly Rods* (2000), "The short rod requires the angler to move his arms either a greater distance or at a faster rate in order to achieve line speeds equivalent to that obtainable with longer rods." Longer rods can help lift more line and make bigger mends. The longer the rod, the greater the radius you can achieve by following or leading your fly downstream. This can increase the length of a float or swing before drag occurs. I like to use a nine to ten-footer for steelhead and salmon. The nine-footer is better for accurate dry fly fishing and the ten-footer is better for high-sticking or swinging. In saltwater, I like nine-foot rods.

Knowing that length increases potential casting distance, the ACA limits the maximum rod length. Rods longer than nine feet also help keep the fly off the ground on backcasts when cast upright. Conversely, longer rods also require more effort to load because of the inefficiency of their leverage. The longer a rod, the more leverage it exerts on the casting hand when held near horizontal because the center of gravity is further away from the fulcrum than in a short rod. Longer rods are not as accurate as shorter ones because small hand errors are amplified out at the tip of long rods. Many of the best ACA accuracy casters have preferred an eight foot six rod rather than a nine-footer. A longer rod usually weighs more too.

Short rods are more maneuverable in brush and cover. Their center of gravity is closer to the handle, which improves tip speed and reduces counterflex. For trout fishing in small streams with trees and tall brush, a six to eight-foot rod is a practical length. For mid to large trout streams, stillwaters, and warmwater fishing, eight and a half to nine feet is a good average.

Some manufacturers design rods of varying lengths with similar action and line weight. To extend length past nine feet, they end up with a larger butt diameter and the rod is a little heavier because of extra material and length and extra guides. There is a fine line between different rod tip actions. It has to be stiff enough to form a tight loop on close casts but if it's too stiff it won't produce much line speed. The tip needs to load adequately in order to operate as a spring. 2014 saw a trend by one manufacturer's seven foot six inch one-piece saltwater rods with stiff tips designed for short heads and ease of casting. Time will tell.

ROD FINISHES

Rod manufacturers started applying shiny finishes to man-made blanks to make them look cosmetically pleasing. Bamboo rods are usually lacquered to seal and protect the natural cane and add to its appearance. Some builders dip blanks in long tubes filled with finish, while others apply finish on a turning machine with a brush. Composite rod builders also found finishing helps prevent impact damage from heavy flies and the resulting warranty costs. The downside to coating is added weight and shine. Some anglers, including me, think wary trout spook from unnecessary rod flash. Some manufacturers had models that were uncoated and a lot of us liked them. The late Tom White, expert casting instructor, suggested I remove the finish on my shiny rods with 0000 steel wool to lighten them for quicker rebound. I have done this successfully. If you remove yours, I wouldn't expect factories to warranty the blanks.

ROD COMPONENTS

Rod components, guides, handles, reel seats, and fighting butts all have variations for different fishing situations. Many manufacturer and consumer decisions are based on appearance or cost and others are based on function. Guides should be durable but reduce friction and reduce tangles. A company named REC Components manufactures everything but the blanks for many of the world's fly rod manufacturers. The biggest innovation in guides has been REC's RECOIL guides made of nickel titanium alloy wire commercially known as Nitinol, one of the "Shape Memory" materials. It is formed in an annealed state and then heat treated, making them hard and wear resistant, yet flexible. For a stripper guide, I have preferred an aluminum oxide ring set in a stainless frame. The smaller contact area of a wire stripper guide makes hauling line a little sticky. REC is in the process of developing a NiTi frame/ceramic ring combination. This new guide will be lighter than traditional stainless frames and have a low friction ceramic ring. This provides the best of both worlds.

The choice in reel seats is more than a matter of cosmetics or weight, it also affects function. Slide-ring seats have minimum weight and elegance and locking-ring seats provide more security when fighting

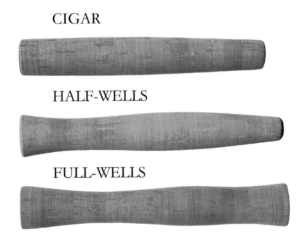

CIGAR

HALF-WELLS

FULL-WELLS

Cork has been the perfect fly rod handle material since it replaced wound rattan at the end of the nineteenth century. The photo shows some of the most popular traditional shapes used today.

big fish. Locking rings are either up-locking or down-locking. Up-locking seats position the reel closer to the handle but require a longer butt below the reel. This is good if you desire a fighting butt. Having a fighting butt makes butt wrapping of the line a possibility. If you don't need a fighting butt and don't mind the reel at the end of the seat, down-locking might be for you. Unfortunately, these are uncommon in production rods and might require a custom build if it's a necessity.

Favorite fly-rod handles are a personal matter but manufacturers have followed a few conventions. They use three main shapes: full wells, reverse half wells (often called Western), and cigar. The idea is, the larger the line weight and the more effort needed for casting or fighting fish, the more thumb support is needed. Therefore, full wells for rods over 7-weight and half wells or cigar for line weights below. If you build a custom handle, you can make any shape, size, or material you want. Some manufacturers use foam for handles and custom builders and owners sometimes use Tourna-Grip or other synthetic wraps over cork or other base. Most people like the feel and tradition of cork. Some old tournament rods had a thumb support on top of the handle shaped from oversized rings or pieces of cork. Portugal still exports the best quality cork but some manufacturers have found more economical supplies of lower grade cork in Korea. The best cork is soft and has the least cracks and pits. Up until recently, most rod manufacturers fitted rod handles sized for large hands. Now I see shorter length and smaller diameter handles on certain presentation models. I think it's a good thing.

CHOOSING RODS AND ROD MAKERS

The casting ability of the angler, as well as the outfits and rigs needed to fish for specific waters and species, dictate how the angler should cast. If you fish in many kinds of places, you will have to use specialized tackle to match each situation. That may include a wide range of rods with lines, leaders, and reels to match. When you're choosing a rod, test cast it with the line of the same weight you're intending to fish with. I usually use a floating line for testing because it has the most air resistance and diameter. Therefore it travels slower than a high-density line and if it is a light color, instead of black, like most high-density lines, I can watch the loops much more easily. If the rod is to be used mainly with sink heads, I'll also try the one I expect will work and see how well it handles it. So if you tested a 4-weight rod and it casts much better with a 5-weight line at about sixty feet, I'd call that a 5-weight rod, despite the marking on the rod.

If you know where and for what you will be fishing, it'll almost point you in the direction of the best tool for the job. Once you establish rod length, action is the primary concern. Stiff rods help catapult heavy wind resistant flies better than soft ones. If you have the strength to cast them, stiff rods of the correct design help with distance and casting in winds since they can help create tight loops and high line speed. Rods with softer action help protect tippet breakage during rod hook sets on smaller species. On most saltwater species, the strip set is the way to go and the tip isn't involved.

When selecting a line weight and rod, the flies I will be casting are my first consideration. I need to take into account the amount of wind resistance and the weight of the flies I'll be using. For example, I love fishing for stripers feeding on giant forage and I use big flies to imitate them. I'll select the line and rod combination to match the flies, which is actually stiffer than I need to fight the fish. I also use stiffer actions if I expect wind, rather than my standard rods for calm conditions. For example I have wonderful 10-weight rods for permit for winds to ten mph and another set of a stiffer action 10-weight, for winds up to twenty. The stiffer ones weigh a little more, or I'd always use them. The lighter action rod would not be able to cast a tight loop into the wind since they tend to overload and bend excessively due to wind drag on the line. I don't recommend going down or up on line size because of wind on a given rod and matching line. For fishing for some species in windy conditions, I might take a heavier outfit, if heavier line weight doesn't compromise presentation.

If it's trout fishing, I ask another question. What fly sizes and tippets am I'm going to use, and how much wind do I expect on the water? I test new rods and assign each a minimum tippet size it can handle without breaking when trout fishing. When I need a 7X rod for a tiny stream, I know which seven-footer to take, or if it's a 4X rod for big flies on big water, which is a nine-footer. I generally use the outfits that weigh the least. I also have my wind rods for trout fishing too. They need to have a stiff enough butt for high line speed but enough softness in the tip to cushion the hook set.

Modern rod technology was a '60s spinoff of aerospace technology on the West Coast. Ex-employees from companies like Lockheed and Boeing in Washington State helped export manufacturing techniques to the rod industry. Early raw materials came from Union Carbide, Hercules Fibers, and later, 3M. Even today, there are little differences in the raw materials and techniques used to make all graphite blanks. Most differences between manufacturers are in the designs. Per Brandin said something to me that I found quite profound: bamboo is a material with constant properties. When new materials appear, as happened recently with Nano-resin technology, the rod designers have to start from scratch! Some manufacturers were successful with this right off the bat, others took a couple of seasons.

Tackle manufacturers need to come out with radically new products every five years or sales go flat. They can't stay in business waiting for tackle to wear out. The tackle manufacturers offer changes in three ways. One way is if anglers show new demand for specific needs, another is the innovation of new materials or engineering designs, and lastly, the industry steers potential customers to new products with PR and merchandising. They tell anglers of the advantage or added value of their new product and to go buy one. Sometimes claims are true and sometimes not. Caveat emptor.

Many anglers are confused by terms used by manufacturers, dealers, instructors, and anglers to describe and mark rods and lines. A good example is when many manufacturers started under-rating rods and line weights around the turn of the millennium when they saw a market for rods with a distance advantage or ability to sling more lead. The line manufacturers responded by making lines from a third to two sizes heavier than the AFTTA standards for their designation. With the use of a stiffer rod, heavier lines assist distance or load easier with rods that do match AFTTA standards. I believe manufacturers also underrate lines (heavier than marked), because they are easier for beginning casters to use at close range; deeper loading is easier to feel and promotes proper timing. The problem with the current AFTTA line standard is the thirty-foot measurement standard. Not all heads are thirty feet and not all casters carry just thirty feet of line. Many anglers and industry people suggest a total grain weight standard for a given rod, such as 540 grains, period. This does seem more logical and relates to our real use of a variety of lines. Rod descriptions can also be misleading.

AFFTA Approved Fly Line Weight Specifications

LINE WEIGHT	TAPERS LOW	TARGET	HIGH	LINE WEIGHT	TAPERS LOW	TARGET	HIGH
	WEIGHT IN GRAINS				WEIGHT IN GRAMS		
1	54	60	66	1	3.50	3.90	4.30
2	74	80	86	2	4.80	5.20	5.60
3	94	100	106	3	6.10	6.50	6.90
4	114	120	126	4	7.40	7.80	8.20
5	134	140	146	5	8.70	9.10	9.50
6	152	160	168	6	9.90	10.40	10.90
7	177	185	193	7	11.50	12.00	12.50
8	202	210	218	8	13.10	13.60	14.10
9	230	240	250	9	14.90	15.55	16.20
10	270	280	290	10	17.50	18.15	18.80
11	318	330	342	11	20.60	21.40	22.20
12	368	380	392	12	23.80	24.60	25.40
13	435	450	465	13	28.20	29.20	30.20
14	485	500	515	14	31.10	32.40	33.70
15	535	550	565	15	34.30	35.60	36.90

WEIGHT IS FOR FIRST 30' OF LINE MINUS LEVEL TIP

These line specs show a weight range for the first thirty feet of line. Use them as a guideline but test a rod to establish its matching line weight in grains. This can be applied to selecting any length head you might need.

How many times have you read about light presentation models of trout fly rods? Or, "A cane rod helps you present a fly with greater delicacy." Using the proper weight matching rod and line, the action of the rod should not affect the delicacy of short-range delivery. Delicacy is determined by the line weight, leader design, and delivery technique. Delivering a light fly softly on target can be accomplished with stiffer actions by using a slow stroke and an aiming point or trajectory permitting the leader to straighten inches above the water. On the other hand, softer rods, especially those softer in the tip, are easier to load at close range and for protecting light tippets. Rod design can also have an affect on rod tracking. If the action of a rod is too parabolic and soft, the rod tip will have more deviation from its casting plane during a stroke. This can cause inaccuracy and bad loops.

Almost every brand of rods has one or several that are superior to its competition. I recommend trying rods of several makers for comparison. Each rod maker has a history that has an influence upon their products and emphasis. Some US rod makers manufacture their rods in the USA and others have them produced in Asia. Here are some examples of how some of the biggest rod manufacturers describe their actions and composition. In alphabetical order:

- **Echo Fly Fishing** designs rods made of medium and fast modulus graphite and glass. They consist of actions described as Glass-M-Fast, Med-Fast, Med-Fast-er, Fast-ish, and Fast. Made in China.

- **G.Loomis** differentiates the actions in their fly rods by describing them from Slow to Extra-Fast and from Moderate to Stiff Power. As they state in their conventional tackle literature, I will assume they mean power is lifting, fighting and casting strength. Their rod materials range from GL to NRX Nano-silica resin technology. Made in the U.S.A.

- **House of Hardy** Fly rods offers a line of rods of nano-technology graphite and resin called Sintrix, and ranges from "middle to tip actions" to fast. Their lower modulus graphite and glass/graphite rods have "easy loading actions." Made in Korea.

- **Orvis Fly Rods** developed The Orvis Flex Index back in the mid-1990s and offered to share it with other manufacturers, but none took them up on the offer. It helps Orvis and its customers relate rod actions within the brand. The Orvis Flex Index: Full Flex 2.5–5.5, Mid Flex 6–9, Tip Flex 9.5–12.5. Made in the U.S.A. and Korea

- **R.L. Winston Rod Co.** describes its rod actions from Slow in bamboo, to Medium to Fast in graphite and from Fast to Super-Fast in their boron series, which uses both graphite and boron. Made in the U.S.A. and China

- **Sage Fly Fishing** offers a range of actions they call "Slow to Ultra fast," plus descriptions like, Smooth, Ultra Light, Ultimate Torque, and Incredible Accuracy. [What material!] Made in the U.S.A.

- **Scott Fly Rod Company** offers hand-built X-Core (Expanded Core), Multi-Modulus graphite, glass, and split-cane rods. They describe their actions from medium slow, medium, medium fast, fast, and very fast. Made in the U.S.A.

- **St. Croix Rods** manufactures all-graphite fly rods and range from moderate to fast action. 3M™ Matrix Resin Nano silica technology. Most of their rods are fast action, with the emphasis of their trout and warm water rods on steamer presentation. Made in the U.S.A. and Mexico.

- **Temple Fork Outfitters** offers rods from medium to fast action and uses a bar chart to show the amount of Presentation, Distance, and Lifting qualities of each model. I see the terms: high modulus, S-glass and IM6 blend, and IM6 as the materials used in their blanks. They are the first to offer Conversion Kits that use alternate components to make a long two-hand rod, or a short one-hand rod. Made in Korea.

Although others have contradicted this, I think waving a rod without a line is a valid way of checking rod action and seeing its counter-flex and recovery characteristics.

REELS

Fly reels serve several simple purposes, but also have an effect on the rod. Ideally, reels store and protect line with a minimum of memory, hold sufficient backing, give auditory feedback with a clicker, and provide a mechanical drag or rim for manual braking. They vary in capacity and diameter, which determines retrieve speed.

The addition of the weight and torque of a reel affects the rod and how it handles. Some anglers debate about the weight balance between rod and reel. Some select reels of sufficient weight to counterbalance their rod to balance near the top of the handle, thinking it would make fishing less tiring. The counterbalancing effect from the weight of a reel

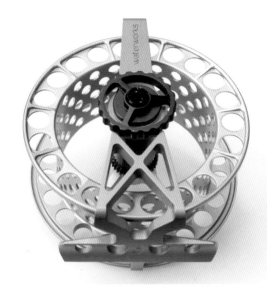

This is the lightest freshwater fly reel on the market. It is a Waterworks Lamson Force SL reel. Some anglers despise light reels, others like me covet them like diamonds. Photo credit John Field

on a rod increases, the closer the rod gets to the horizontal position. So, if you do "high-stick nymphing" all day with a ten-foot rod, you might be concerned about rod balance. Of course this balance will change when there is less line on the reel when line is extended and being used. Unfortunately, the higher the total combined weight of the reel and rod, the harder it is to hold all day and slower and more difficult it is to swing. I contend it's better to swing a lighter outfit all day with a reel that doesn't counterbalance the rod, than to cast the same rod with a heavier weight reel on it, just for balance.

The larger the spool side diameter, the more its torque affects the rod when cast with the reel toward the outside of your casting hand. Less weight reduces that effect.

The two modern methods of manufacturing the main parts of fly reels are casting or machining them from billet or stock. A manufacturer can achieve a lighter reel of the same or greater strength by machining, since they can machine heat-treated aluminum. This is much stronger than cast aluminum, which is not heat-treated. You can therefore remove more material by hollowing it within limits and still retain strength. The strength of cast aluminum is lower, so you need to use more of it to withstand use. With the advantages of machining comes higher cost. The greater the arbor diameter of a reel, the less line memory it will keep. The wider the spool, the greater the percentage of line wound at a larger diameter. Therefore that spool will reduce memory compared to a narrow one. A more constant diameter also helps a drag system give more consistent resistance, as the distance a fish runs increases. Large diameter spools provide a quicker retrieve when fighting fast running fish.

Drags have three major designs and several material variations to provide resistance. First, an adjustable click-and-pawl prevents overrun and provides a minimal drag for the lightest tippets. Secondly, a disc drag system with a disc affixed to the frame and another that rotates with the spool. Third, a conical drag which uses one stationary and a rotating cone drag element, one inside the other to bear against each other. The last two both use a threaded tensioner-knob to adjust pressure. The conical drag is lighter, but has not proven to dissipate heat as well as the greater surface area of disc drags.

FLY LINES

The first fishing lines were multi-purpose and made of twisted horse hair and tapered in an effort to decrease the weight and diameter of the end of the line so it didn't hit the water so hard and was not as visible. A byproduct of this taper was also the dissipation of energy. This also made presentation more delicate. Silk line enthusiasts in the 1800s and manufacturers of tapered coating lines in the 1950s began experimenting with taper designs at both ends of the fly line and discovered their properties. Full commercial floating fly

Today's manufacturers offer a full gamut of densities, sizes, and colors from glow-in-the-dark, Day-Glo, to camouflage
Photo credit John Field

lines for hand rods today range in length from 85 to 120 feet. AFTTA, the American Fly Tackle Trade Association, has published the current industry standard for fly line weights (see chart on p. 113). This standard is the weight of the first thirty feet of fly line. Many heads are longer than that and weigh much more than the standard. Since the standard doesn't take into consideration carrying more line in the air than thirty feet, many anglers unknowingly overload their rods.

LINE TAPER

The basic fly line is level, un-tapered, or of relatively constant diameter. You can directly connect a level fly line to a leader or shooting line of greatly differing diameters. The use of a level line will result in fast loop turnover and a short flight. A level line, leader and fly will fall harder onto the water than a tapered line. Level line can be used for "chuck and duck" fishing which is a technique of throwing heavy flies or fly-and-sinker combinations for anadromous fish in rivers.

FLY LINE TAPERS

Level Taper—L

Double Taper—DT

Weight Forward Taper with integrated running line—WF

Weight Forward Compound Taper with integrated running line—WF

Shooting head (tapered) and Shooting line—SH

Triangle Taper with integrated running line

Each different type of taper and each specific line design is aimed at a specific application. Knowing how to select them can give you great control over your casting and angling.

Taper is a change of diameter of a fly line to reduce its visibility and change its distribution of mass, which affects energy dissipation. This reduction of energy and diameter down the line and leader to the fly determines the rate of turnover and how hard they land on the water. The shapes of today's tapers are elongated cones of varying angles and lengths and can be combined to form compound tapers. The first six inches to a foot of a fly line is a level tip intended to provide consumable length for making leader connections without getting into the larger diameter taper. The front taper has an effect on the rate and force of loop turnover. The shorter the taper, the quicker and more forcefully the loop will open. Short tapers can open heavy leaders with heavy flies and deal with wind better than long ones. But they lack delicacy. Long distance lines will have a normal front taper around five feet. The belly is the next line section and usually contains the majority of mass and greatest diameter. The belly is usually level except at least in the case of the Wulff Triangle Taper and the compound saltwater tapers of Scientific Anglers. A long belly also delays loop turnover and is good for a distance line. The longer the head, the longer it takes to straighten. This makes the line more subject to gravity. Therefore, the longer the head, the more likely the fly will tick the water. An integrated line is one piece comprised of a head and thinner running line built on a continuous core. It may be one density, or made of several coatings of differing densities. A shooting head is sold as an interchangeable component that requires a separate shooting line to be attached with a handshake loop. Heads and shooting lines can be purchased in varying densities.

A double-taper line has one level belly and a taper and tip at each end, like a mirror image. The double taper is reversible if worn or damaged, to increase its useful life. When you cast a double taper, the belly is always in the rod tip, which helps load the rod for roll casts, Spey casts and mends. You know the adage: you can't turn over heavier line with lighter line. The lack of a running-line makes shooting less efficient with a double taper. Also, since the AFTTA standard line weight is at a thirty-foot length, you are theoretically over-lining your rod when you cast a double taper beyond that length.

A weight-forward line has a tip, front taper, belly, rear taper, and running line. Some manufacturers even use a compound taper in their design. I've used this design most to help rod loading for short casts. A rear taper helps smooth out the transition between the head diameter and a much thinner diameter running line. The rear taper also extends the working length of line when it is used for making roll, or Spey casts. When making these casts, you need the mass of thicker line near the rod tip to move the belly and load the rod if the running line is too light.

A thinner level line is used as running line, since it presents less resistance when hauling or shooting. You extend the running line past the tip to extend the amount of line in the air beyond the head and control loop turnover. With a given rod, there is a maximum overhang of running line you can false cast before waves form in the loop and deteriorate its effectiveness. A head turns over better with a running line that has sufficient drag, just as a kite needs a tail. That is one-reason manufacturers don't simply use mono as a running line.

The Triangle Taper developed by Lee Wulff has a continuous forward taper in the head for the first twenty-seven to forty feet, depending on the application. It is designed with the heavier line constantly turning over the lighter line. The weight is farther away from the leader than in any other tapered line and so it is good for delicate presentations. With more weight rearward, it is good for roll and Spey casts. I noted this line is increasing in popularity in Europe when I was fishing there.

The most important choice in a weight-forward or triangle-tapered fly line for distance is head length. The more line you can carry, the longer you can cast. If your backcast hits the ground or water behind you no matter what trajectory you attempt, you can't carry that much line. Since maximum line carriage increases distance, long-head lines (greater than forty-two feet) are the best for distance and for other aforementioned reasons, best for long roll and Spey casts too. When using a floating line, you can probably shoot a maximum of about forty feet. So to cast 100, you must carry sixty. If you want to win a 5-weight shootout with a 120-foot SA (Scientific Anglers) MED line (Mastery Expert Distance), you'll need to carry eighty and shoot at least forty!

Anglers and pundits debate which line is a more practical fishing tool for trout fishing, a double-taper or weight-forward. The double-taper advocates say its continuous belly makes long, water-anchored casts and mends possible. They also like the option of reversing an old or damaged line. Weight-forward advocates say shooting line is easier with their line and they can make waterborne casts up to fifty feet, including the leader. That's only with WF line with a forty-foot head. They also say the WF line is lighter on the reel and doesn't take up as much space. Unlike the double-taper, you will often have the thinner running line in the guides. This does two things. First, it helps cast tighter loops, since less weight is in the guides and rod tip. Secondly, the thinner, lighter line double-hauls through the guides more easily.

After much testing with both the weight forward and the double taper for my dry fly fishing, I choose WF. The heads on WF floating lines are long enough to perform my mends, rolls, Speys, and longest fishing casts, and hauling with them is superior. I haul to increase line speed to battle wind, dry-off flies, and increase casting distance. I can't haul nearly as fast with the heavier, thicker belly of a double taper in my guides. I do recommend using dull colored lines or those with a camo tip for spooky fish. I try not to false cast over fish at all costs. I think the flash of the reflection of sun on lines is what spooks fish most. Using a long leader also helps keep the silhouette of the line further away from the fish.

In integrated lines, you can select line with full-floating to full-sinking densities and almost infinite tip and belly combinations. Integrated lines go through the guides the easiest, but can be limiting if you need to change anything. To change line requires changing a reel with another line or changing the entire line. With a shooting-head system, you might not have as many options for the single hand rod as an integrated line, but you can change them individually in short order. For example, you can change the density of a head from Intermediate 2 to Sinking 7 in a minute with a minimum of things to carry. You have more running line options when you select a shooting head system. Some are much thinner and longer than those on integrated lines and can add distance to your casts. Intermediate running lines are also available. The downside is the handshake loop connectors are annoying to pass through the guides and they have to be maintained and lines replaced to prevent breakage. I lost one of the biggest stripers I've ever hooked when a rear head loop failed and the striper swam away with the head, probably to its eventual death. When I asked the distributor about the failure, he said, I'll send you a new one, but you should replace them every five years. I said, you should have told me last year!

CONSTRUCTION AND DENSITY

Lines are constructed with a core for strength and a coating to give them weight and desired density. The two most common line coatings today are PVC (Poly Vinyl Cloride) and Polyethelene. The cores inside today's fly lines are braided Kevlar, Dacron and monofilament nylon and single strand monofilament nylon. Scientific Anglers has redesigned and reintroduced textured line coatings in the interest of higher floatation and distance. Their engineers say the texture traps air for higher floatation and the texture reduces surface area, thus reducing friction.

The biggest improvement in lines has been the new low-stretch material used in their cores. The less stretch the core has, the better it casts and transmits energy and vibration. Scientific Anglers' Bruce Richards and Airflo distributor, Tim Rajeff, discussed this in the article "How Does Stretch Affect the Cast?" in IFFF's The Loop, Winter 2002. Some manufacturers use no-stretch Kevlar cores. We have all known about the super-braid revolution that took place in the '90s, but it took this long for fly line manufacturers to successfully use that material in a fly line with reliability. The problem up to now was, the coatings wouldn't stay on the core. This core has a better strength-to-diameter ratio, provides more sensitivity, and has less stretch.

Rio Fly Lines recently released their new ConnectCore low-stretch line with 6 percent stretch compared to the 30 percent of previous materials.

Some line coatings adhere to the core so well, they won't slip and others can easily be slid off with your fingernails. I like fairly hard glossy finishes. I'm not a lover of textured lines. I like silence from my tackle. I liked the original Airflo Ridge lines, but other textured lines make an annoying sound moving through the guides and damage the skin on your fingers. In distance testing, the Scientific Anglers Sharkskin GPX against the regular GPX, there is a slight distance advantage. Most of today's fly lines have welded loops at both ends. On Spey lines or in some saltwater situations, that's a liability. If you reel the connection through the guides, it can cost you a fish. I often use fourteen-foot trout leaders, and a fly line tip-connection loop does not pass easily through my guides when I try netting my fish.

I recommend using a nail-knot to join the butt section of a leader to a fly line for lines from 12-weight down to 6-weight. Below that, I recommend a needle-nail knot. You can use five turns for a 5-weight, four for a 4-weight and three for a 3 and smaller. You can also attach a short piece of mono to the fly line butt with these connections and a perfection loop on the end to attach to a loop in your leader. The type of coating, how well it is bonded, and the core, determines what the strongest connection should be. Just remember, you can't perform a needle nail-knot on line cores unless they are hollow. For my two-hand Spey lines, I've learned how to make welded plastic loops with a heat gun and shrink tubing as a form. I don't make my steelhead Spey leaders longer than the rod and since I don't reel the connection into the guides, loops aren't a problem. For big freshwater species and saltwater fish up to about 100 pounds, a regular nail-knot works. For big saltwater fish I use a double nail-knot loop, or insert the line in an eighteen-inch long piece of fifty-pound braid with a loop at the other end.

Once you know the matching line weight for the rod you want to use, the line density is the next choice. Choices are from full-floating, in freshwater or saltwater density, through full-sinking Type 8. Lines are available in constant density or several density combinations of tip, belly, head, and running lines.

My two primary considerations in choosing a sinking line are the sink rate and the angle of retrieve for the length of the cast. Weight being equal, a longer sinking head will be retrieved at a lesser angle than a shorter tip or belly. In saltwater fishing, I usually don't want a line to sink greater than at a 45-degree angle in order for the retrieve to look natural. Therefore, I choose a sinking head or full sink, twice the length of the depth I'm trying to reach. If you're drifting in a boat in wind or current, the sink rate should be selected to achieve the desired depth as quickly as possible. If I'm trying to graze bottom in fifteen feet of water, a sinking head of thirty feet will be fine. If I'm trying to catch weakfish or Jack Crevalle down forty-five feet and the tide and wind aren't too bad, I use my full sink ninety-foot line with some additional mono running line, stack mend it and count it down! A thirty-foot 10-weight floating head might be .070" in diameter, a 10-weight Intermediate might be .050" thick and Type 7 full sink, might be .040".

So the higher the density, all things being equal, the thinner the line and the less its wind resistance when cast. That's why tournament sanctioning bodies like ACA and ICSF specify thin, high-density heads for their official distance lines for maximum distance. Here's a tip I learned from Captain Jaime Boyle of Martha's Vineyard: Use an intermediate line to throw poppers in saltwater instead of a floating line. The intermediate casts farther because it's denser, and it will sink through waves a little instead of floating on the top of them. This will help prevent slack and make popping a fly like my favorite, the Gurgler, a bit easier.

Fly line trends in the 2000s have been toward shorter heads and underrated or heavier physical weight than designated. Sinking heads used to be as long as forty-five feet. My favorites were thirty-five feet long. Now the trend is back to thirty feet and getting shorter.

FLY LINE AND ROD CARE

Fly line performance deteriorates from the accumulation of dirt and from twists and coil memory. Current, forward boat motion, and stripping can cause a fly to spin. A weed on the hook can cause line-damaging twists. Mending in one direction will also put twist in the line. Storing line on the reel for long periods, especially in high temperatures, will create coil memory. Having an unnecessary snarl ruin a cast to a fish you've invested time in, is a disappointing waste. That's why I'm a fanatic about line cleanliness, straightness, and storage. It improves casting immeasurably. If a line has coil memory, you must stretch it out before casting. Trailing a line behind a boat will straighten twists as long as nothing on the end causes it to spin. When I fished in Florida every month for five years, I would stop over and see my parents at each end of the trip. I would wait till after midnight and hang my fly lines off the balcony of the 22nd floor of their high-rise building. so they could straighten under their own weight. I often envisioned a displeased resident would cut my line with a pair of scissors. I believe in washing floating saltwater lines every couple of days with mild soap and water and lubricating them. I still use Glide on all my floating lines. Even though almost all modern fly lines are self-lubricating, I do it anyway. Rods and reels also need periodic care.

When you finish for the day in saltwater, rinse the rods down with a hose at close range, but spare the pressure on the reels. A light sprinkle is all that's needed to help dissolve most of the salt and rinse away sand, etc. Driving contamination into bearings and drags is not a good idea. Once a week I remove the reels and wash them with mild soap, warm water, and a terry-cloth. I rinse out the cloth and wipe and re-rinse until the suds are gone. I annually clean my rod by rubbing the guides and feet with WD-40 on a Q-Tip and spraying the reel seat with it and wiping it dry with a paper towel too. I wipe the male ferrule with a clean paper towel and apply ferrule wax directly and buff it in with the tip of my index finger. Always check the tightness of your ferrules after a lot of casts. Casting a rod with loose ferrules can damage them.

Storing line tightly on the reel from your last trip can make it difficult to cast for the first few hours of your next trip. The line coating can conform to the shape of the line under it and leave dents and flat spots. Prevent this after your next trip by stripping-out the line and wind it on with little tension. Use a line-winder and remove lines you won't be using for a long time, bind them with pieces of twisted pipe cleaner, and store each one in a Ziploc bag. I only use silver or gold anodized reels instead of dark colors, so they don't heat-up in the sun and I don't leave lines in a hot vehicle.

To insure the leader and line work together well, leader design is very important. The leader is vital since it's the closest part of your tackle to the fish.

LEADERS

The attributes of a leader depend on the species you're targeting and the conditions you're fishing in. The leader might be required to hide the fly and the line, transfer energy from the cast so it turns over, and provide slack or bite protection. You can even compensate for an absent or inadequate front taper in the fly line with leader design. The design variables to select from are its dimensions, taper, materials, and construction.

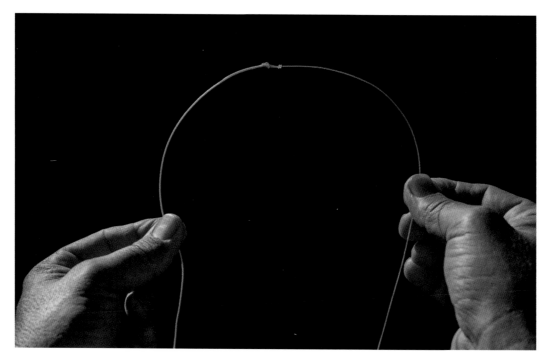

The test for proper leader butt material selection is testing the relative flexibility of line and butt after they are joined.

Nylon and fluorocarbon are today's two leader material choices. I opt for nylon for freshwater floating presentations, but will use a fluorocarbon tippet or replace the tippets of worn knotless nylon leaders with fluorocarbon without worries of losing the floating properties of the fly. Nylons from different brands and selections can vary greatly in stiffness and you should use this to your advantage when designing a leader. For example, in the brand Maxima, there are three nylon leader materials, Clear, Ultra Green, and Chameleon. They are in order from limpest to stiffest. You can even combine more than one type in a leader. If you go to the trouble of making a hand-made tapered leader, it's smart to measure all materials with a micrometer beforehand and remark the spool if it varies from the manufacturers' stated thickness. The marked diameter of monofilament is notoriously inaccurate because of production variances. The breaking strength is often understated to be on the safe side and give anglers heightened satisfaction with their products. Line-to-leader connections, as well as leader-butt selection, should not cause hinging or excessive stiffness. Poor leader connections can interrupt the energy transfer from the line to the leader through hinging or excessive stiffness.

Unless you're fishing with a guide, you really have to tie your own saltwater leaders. For saltwater fish, I almost always use fluorocarbon. Fluorocarbon is stellar because it has much higher abrasion resistance than nylon with a greater strength-to-diameter ratio. Therefore, an angler can use thinner tipper diameters when stealth counts. When it first came out, I tried to cut a tag end with my teeth like I used to with nylon. It was so hard it hurt!

In saltwater applications, I connect leader sections with a blood knot or double nail knot and attach flies with a uni-knot or loop knot. I use a bimini twist and double surgeon's loop in the top of the leader to connect to a loop in the fly line or extension with a hand-shake loop. When I need a heavy wire bite-tippet in salt, I use a wire twister and form a neat, round loop in single strand stainless and tie fluorocarbon directly to one end and connect the fly with a haywire twist. For freshwater and surface flies in salt, I'll attach a tie-able flexible wire with a double nail knot connection to a fluorocarbon leader and connect the fly with a loop knot.

In designing a leader, it's best to design them only as long and as fine as they have to be, in order to prevent spooking your prey. The shorter they are, the easier they are to cast. For sinking lines and streamers for example, you can get away with leaders half as long as you might need to use for surface presentations. Sometimes however, there's a limit how short you can make a leader, since a short leader opens earlier than a long one and can kick downward. If your cast is made low, this can tick the water during false casts and scare fish. Steve Rajeff also taught me to design a tournament-casting leader that doesn't tick, since it's a deduction.

Even tippet length adjustments when trout fishing can affect leader turnover rate and slack. I use a pocket thickness gauge for rigging and for building a leader or checking the taper or tippet. Tying knots and snagging limbs consume tippet so it's inevitable you'll need to add some more. A 60-20-20 percent split between butt, middle, and tippet length is a basic leader formula for use on floating lines. Sizing the nylon or fluorocarbon butt section at 66 percent of the diameter of the fly line tip will provide good energy transfer for turning over the leader. No matter whether you're using nylon or fluorocarbon, you can make an S shape in your tippet if you'd like by experimenting with its length. You'll know when your tippet is too long when it lands in a tangle despite a good cast.

George Daniel's book, *Dynamic Nymphing* (2012), describes French and Spanish nymphing using long leaders, such as the Hends Camou French leader. It comes in a 3- or 9-meter length. These techniques are aimed at presenting one or two nymphs to trout and grayling in shallow, clear water using a sight indicator. Sight indicators, or sighters, are sections of highly visible mono tied or looped into the leader. The object is to locate the sighter just above the water for best visibility. Anglers using this long a leader only let out a foot or two of fly line past the tip. To cast this monstrosity, I recommend using a nice, straight stroke and let the leader straighten. Instead of your all-around trout rod, a specialized ten-foot, number three or four rod will help cast the long leaders and help keep as much line off the water as possible to prevent drag.

There is a divide among the experts over leader design in regard to drag. Drag is generally scorned when using dry flies and nymphs in dead-drift presentations. Some say the leader should land straight and slack should be added to the fly line, others say the leader should land in soft curves and the line doesn't matter much. I don't think soft curves in a leader ensure a drag-free drift. I think slack in the line is more important. I experimented with George Harvey's drag-free leader formulas and found that slow tapers with smaller butt diameters do not turn over well. Also, when a leader with soft curves drags on the water, the fly follows the curves of the tippet across the water.

I used to take pride in designing and tying my own trout leaders, but modern knotless tapered leaders work better. Knotless leaders are visually less intrusive, don't collect substances like algae, and, lacking knots, they seem to be less prone to tangling. The fourteen-foot knotless nylon leaders I use from Trouthunter have the right butt stiffness and length and turn over remarkably well.

FIELD TIP

In fly fishing, choosing, testing, combining, and tuning the right components can create well-matched equipment and prepare you for the field. This will help you be more efficient in performing casts and fishing more intuitively. The ultimate goal in fly casting is to learn the feel of all types of fly rods and line combinations, and if presented with an unfamiliar outfit, adapt your stroke to make good casts. You might be asked to do it in front of an audience.

Whenever I see coil memory or kinking in a leader, I stretch the sections between my hands with a loose wrap so the grip doesn't add kinks. The closer you come to the breaking point for each section, the more effective the stretch is. Knotless leaders also make straightening easy by pinching the line between thumb and index finger and slowly creating heat by pulling down the leader toward the end. Maintain the stretch for a few seconds so the leader can cool, then release. A straight leader prevents the fly from springing like a jack-in-the-box and piling.

When you take a knotless tapered leader out to uncoil it, there is a simple way to prevent a snarl. Put the fingers of your line hand inside the coil to act as a spool and start unrolling the butt end and use the straightening directions below until the whole leader is ready.

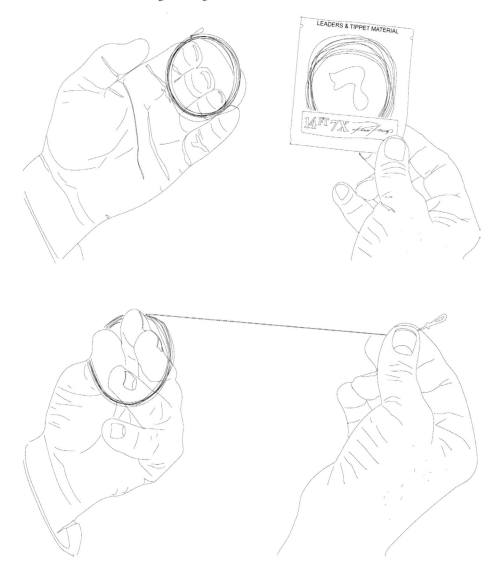

There is nothing more confounding than putting knots in a knotless leader before you even get it attached.

CHAPTER 8

THE FLY CASTING UNIVERSE

Wherever I fish in far-off places or continue my lifelong quest to learn more about fly casting and fishing, I encounter a diversity of techniques and opinions. This localization is usually due to cultural, linguistic, and socioeconomic differences. Fly-fishing preferences and focus are usually formed due to geographic location, species availability (both native and invasive), habitat, and climate. In English, throwing a fly line is a "cast" but in Latin-based languages like Italian and Spanish, the word is "lancia," which translates as launch. In English, we launch rockets and projectiles and we cast, or throw, a dock or fly line. Casting and fishing tactics often evolve out of local necessity. On the small, brushy streams of Italy, casts evolved as a way of casting under overhanging brush and a casting academy was born from it (See TLT Academy p. 133). Traditional Spey casting with two-handed rods was born in Scotland to deal with long swings while fishing for big salmon. Shooting-head, one-handed distance casting evolved on the Pacific coast of America to reach steelhead in medium-sized rivers. It's always an education traveling to fish and learn these adaptations and think of new ways to apply them in other waters.

The Internet has helped casting instructors and anglers share techniques and experiences across the globe. Some of it's helpful, other bits, not so much, to put it mildly. The organizations and blogs I later mention have boards and forums to help you satisfy your quest for knowledge. The more people you share with, the more you will learn about casting. You can also discover wonderful fish, places, people, and different cultures of far-off lands. Through my hard effort to learn, I've become part of an inquisitive group of international fly casting geeks still performing, analyzing, and sharing casting studies to help us cast and teach more effectively. Most of us are looking forward to the release of tackle innovations and some of our group are the ones who do the research and development for the manufacturers. If you're passionate about advancing your casting, you will have to qualify the sources of instruction and information to get the best results.

It would be ideal if all English-tongued fly casting instructors, and books, and videos in English, used the same names and descriptions of casts, taught them, analyzed, and corrected faults the same way. If there would be universal agreement of casting terms, it would enable a student to quickly understand instruction from instructors from different parts of the country and different schools at home and abroad. Unfortunately, as in many sports, there is no standardization of nomenclature and teaching methodology. There may even be major disagreements between different schools on the understanding of a sport's mechanics and its underlying physics. Traditional thinking is very persistent and it's hard for people to have their assumptions challenged. A lot of literature out there about fly casting and angling is becoming obsolete, but still has historical significance. Ego is another reason we have varying definitions and explanations for casting terms. Some experts have the need to brand their own names and methods to differentiate themselves from their competition.

Learning to fly cast can be difficult because of the personality and experiences of instructors that gives them their personal viewpoint or paradigm. Students also have individual ways of learning because of how they are wired. So the way one teacher teaches might be effective for some students and not effective for others. Some people learn to cast by mimicking an instructor, some can learn by listening to an explanation, and others learn by feel. Therefore, instructors should match their methodology with the personality and learning style of the student.

Mel Krieger is famous for recognizing these differences and individualizing instruction for the "poet" vs. the "engineer." He was a poet and offered ways to feel a cast or describe it more viscerally. I have tried to present the concepts and instruction in this book for both types. Ideally, a caster or angler should have at least a working understanding of how casts are made and know the most common jargon and names used by the major influences on modern casting. In explaining these influences, I'll even start from the beginning to offer some historical context.

CASTING PARADIGMS: INTERNATIONAL SCHOOLS, CLUBS, AND ORGANIZATIONS

In America during the nineteenth and early twentieth centuries, the most popular way of learning fly casting and developing new tackle was through clubs and tournament casting. Upper-class Americans also traveled to Europe to fish for trout, grayling, and salmon and were exposed to European casting and fishing techniques at clubs and schools in Switzerland, Austria, and England. One of these Americans was Charles Ritz, who named and described the HS/HL (high speed/high line) casting technique. Charles finalized the documentation of this technique after seeing San Francisco tournament caster Jon Tarantino cast. Mr. Ritz was amazed at how similar Tarantino's casting was to the ideal of his own technique.

In 1907 the National Association of Scientific Angling Clubs (NASAC) was formed. The name was later changed to National Association of Angling and Casting Clubs (NAACC). In 1961 it was changed to American Casting Association, or ACA. The national body became less interested in the games emulating fishing, and focused more into the casting games of the international competition. These organizations have sanctioned the National Casting Championships and the National Casting Records in the US and Canada. The ACA is a member of the ICSF (International Casting Sport Federation) that Cliff Netherton of Virginia and Myron Gregory of California founded in 1955. It started with fourteen national federations and now has twenty-one. The ICSF now competes on grass only and uses water filled accuracy targets.

According to my conversations with the oldest remaining tournament casters, the sport waned because of the advent of spinning tackle and popularity of angling travel by both auto and air. Cliff Netherton revitalized the aging NAACC-certified casting instructor program for the ACA with the assistance of the University of Michigan in the early 1960s through the 1970s. Because of these clubs, casters like Jon Tarantino, Phil Miravelli, Tony Perry, Doug Merrick, Ted Halvorsen, Myron Gregory, and others passed on the old lessons to a new generation. They included Steve Rajeff, Tim Rajeff, Chris Korich, and others.

The Angler's Lodge of the Golden Gate Angling and Casting Club, from the center of the casting pool, at the 100th Annual National Casting Championships. This is where the boys—Chris Korich, Tim Rajeff, and Steve Rajeff—spent much of their youth mastering casting and winning tournaments. Photo Credit John Field

These three grew up around the GGACC, (Golden Gate and Angling and Casting Club) and were forced to learn casting by the old-timers to prevent their teenage mischief around the public grounds of the club. The old-timers, called the "Dirty Dozen," would sit on a bench in "Horner's Corner," named after club member Jack Horner, at the far end of the pools talking about them behind their backs. It wasn't long before all three were beating them.

Chris, Tim, and Steve dominated US and international casting and set dozens of records. Steve is forty-one-time ACA Grand All-Around Champion and has earned a living as Senior Rod Designer for G.Loomis in Washington State. Tim got bored with the same old games, chased fish in Russia and elsewhere, until he founded Rajeff Sports. He owns and operates Echo Fly Fishing and distributes Airflo Fly lines on this continent. He humorously calls himself a casting geek. Chris Korich invented a ski boot and binding tuning system and founded a company called Biostance to develop and market it. He's pretty busy till the ski season is over.

Since the 1990s, Chris Korich, ACA Hall of Fame Member of the Oakland Casting Club, has been the casting coach behind the scenes for the latest champions. He trained the world champion and ACA Distance and Accuracy Record holder, Henry Mittel, and the fast-handed Rene Gillbert, who also holds a few records. Chris has coached many others in varying amounts, including his latest, a ten-year-old girl named Maxine McCormick. Maxine can now beat half the adults in several games! By the time you read this, she could be the next women's champion. Chris has given himself the nickname, the "Casting Jedi." Correspondingly, *Fly Fisherman Magazine* editor Ross Purnell named forty-one-time National Grand Champion Steve Rajeff, "the Terminator of tournament casting." The ACA is currently trying to expand its clubs and preserve and display its rich past for future generations.

THE INTERNATIONAL FEDERATION OF FLY FISHERS

The FFF was founded in 1964 by conservation-minded American fly fishers from coast to coast, spearheaded by the MacKensie Fly Fishers of Eugene, Washington. It was founded for the purpose of conserving and protecting our waters and fish. It has had such growth around the world, it was renamed the International Federation of Fly Fishers in 2013. IFFF is comprised of almost 14,000 members from fifteen councils and sixty charter clubs in the US and hosts the annual International Fly Fishing Fair. The website offers fly fishing, tying, and casting information as well as instructional books and DVDs. Education and their casting instructors are two of their biggest strengths.

Chris Korich of the Oakland Casting Club is passing on his efficient casting technique to many new casters. Photo by Chris Korich.

In 1992, Mel Krieger, a GGACC legend and FFF Executive Committee member at the time, saw an opportunity to help the FFF by proposing a new Casting Instructor Certification Program at FFF. He asked Steve Rajeff of G.Loomis Fly Rods if he and his company would administer the program. Steve declined, saying that if a commercial entity ran the program, it would not be in the public's interest. FFF formed the Casting Board of Governors (B.O.G.) to create the requirements for instructors and the curriculum. In 2014 the BOG passed the Examiner Development Pathway, or EDP, which is a comprehensive quality-assurance program requiring continuing training and record keeping by the examiners to qualify to examine for one of more of the three levels for CI (Casting Instructor), MCI (Master Casting Instructor), and THCI (Two-Hand Casting Instructor).

Bill and Jay Gammel, Joan Salvato Wulff, Mel Krieger, and later Bruce Richards have had the most influence on the casting program's curriculum. The Gammels wrote the book

Essentials of Fly Casting (1993), which has served as a fundamental casting text since its release. Joan and her late husband Lee Wulff, started the Wulff Fly Fishing School in 1979 and she has served on the FFF Casting Board of Governors. Joan has written three books on fly casting and was a child and adult tournament casting star before turning pro. Mel Krieger taught fly casting at home and abroad for twenty-five years and wrote *The Essence of Flycasting* (2001).

Bruce Richards was the chief line designer for Scientific Anglers for many years until his retirement and returned as a consultant after Orvis purchased it from 3M in 2013. Bruce wrote the book titled *Modern Fly Line* (1994), and co-developed the Casting Analyzer (see p. 12) that has helped give us a better understanding of casting physics and mechanics. In addition, he coauthored casting physics studies with Dr. Noel Perkins, Professor of Mechanical Engineering. Bruce is currently a member of the IFFF Casting Board of Governors.

Dr. Gordy Hill ready to catch another striper. Photo courtesy of Gordy Hill

The Definitions Committee headed by Dr. Gordy Hill to whom I've dedicated this book, was formed around the new millennium to try and standardize casting vocabulary, but there were too many disagreements for a majority to adopt one set of terms. It's a work in progress. Gordy is a brilliant and diplomatic man who gives the most articulate and accurate explanations of any person I've had the fortune of knowing. At eighty-three years young, he is the rare, intellectually-passionate angler, who is always inquisitive and advances our collective knowledge every day. Gordy believes a teacher who knows how things work in the scientific sense knows the fundamentals to distill ideas into plain language for teaching. He also believes this prepares the instructor for accurate analysis and new discoveries.

In 2006, Gordy created the MCI Study Group to help Master Casting Instructor candidates prepare for the exam and hone the way they and experienced MCI colleagues teach. This group has been comprised of around 400 IFFF instructors from around the world and has communicated through an email system Gordy ran and paid for himself. Gordy originated and moderated discussion topics, questions, and responses he exchanged with the group. Some physicists and engineers in the Master Study Group have been instrumental in expanding our understanding of casting. They include Bruce Richards, Walter Simburski, Ally Gowen, Server Sadik, Bill Keister, and others.

After fourteen years in 2014, Gordy passed the task of moderator to Walter Simbirski. Walter has divided the discussions into two groups. The main group will consist of MCI candidates preparing for the exam and instructors discussing the process. The second group will be the casting geeks discussing the physics and theory of casting. Today the organization is growing thanks to donations, dues, and volunteers like Gordy and hundreds more.

At about the same time, the educational programs of the U.S. casting clubs and conservation organizations were developing, Europeans were developing their own programs, ideologies, and techniques.

Paul Arden, originally from England, has lived, fished, and taught around the globe. He operates his fly-fishing website and tackle brand called Sexyloops. The site's content is comprised of one-hand fly rod casting and fishing instruction, tackle information, and some conservation. After I shared a good night's fishing with Paul, he mentioned he was late for the Friday front-page deadline on the topic of conservation and asked if I'd write it instead that night! I wrote an essay on my iPhone on the effects of overfishing and he titled it, *Choices*. In addition to Paul's high degree of expertise, some very elite casters are online article contributors to Sexyloops, and are present on his forums. Paul has conducted and analyzed high-speed video and has provided some good "outside the box" results in the interpretation of loop formation, mechanics, and casting semantics.

Seven partners founded CNL Comisión Nacional de Lanzado (Flycasting National Committee of Spain) in 2001 in Madrid. Mel Krieger was the founder of the program called Programa Avanzado de Instructores de Lanzado (PAIL) and examiner of the first instructors. Today, six Pro Staff Instructors who are also IFFF Master and Certified Casting Instructors operate CNL. PAIL has three levels of certifications with an ascending order of requirements. PAIL has twenty instructors designated as Master, six Master Advanced, and twelve Instructors.

EFFA EUROPEAN FLY FISHING ASSOCIATION

Günter Feuerstein, a former FFF Master Casting Instructor, founded EFF in 2006 under Swiss law. Since then, he's become an internationally-known EFFA Master Fly-Casting Instructor and chairman of the EFFA Fly-Casting Instructor Program. EFFA has members in twenty-four countries. Günter, originally from Austria, moved to Switzerland about twenty years ago. This organization has a training and certification program for EFFA Flycasting Instructor, EFFA Master, Flycasting Instructor, EFFA Doublehand Flycasting Instructor, and EFFA Flyfishing Guide. One purpose of this association is to foster conservation. EFFA has an online fly-fishing glossary, two-hand (underhand) casting articles, fishing articles, and fly-casting videos on its website. The EFFA website also states why they parted ways with the FFF:

Early in 2006, the FFF attempted to force their affiliated European partner, FFF-Europe—which was until then independent—to exclusively apply the American standards of flycasting instruction (which are not up to the same standards as the instruction offered in Europe) in their instructors' tests, and to submit all revenue from examinations and membership fees to the American FFF . . .

I've been told that it's probably an even bet whether someone could pass the Masters exam or obtain Swiss naturalization. For example, a candidate is required to flawlessly false cast twenty-four meters without hauling, which is almost eighty feet! The Theoretical Part of the Master test covers fishing and tackle knowledge in deeper depth than required by the IFFF Masters exam. EFFA has twenty-one Masters and sixty-five Basic Instructors.

Günter states on his website he invented the snap-T, the magic switch, the dunker, and several other casts. It is my understanding his casting has been greatly influenced by the techniques of Hans Gebetsroither of Austria, and Göran Andersson of Sweden. Hans Gebetsroither is credited with creating the Belgian cast and used a distal grip. Göran Andersson originated the underhand two-hand casting technique.

AAPGAI

The Association of Advanced Professional Game Angling Instructors, was founded in 2003 by Ally Gowen of Scotland. Fly-fishing lessons, casting instruction, and fly-dressing instruction is given by qualified instructors of three grades; Provisional, Advanced, and Master. They can be qualified in the three disciplines: One-Hand Rod, Two-Hand Rod, and Fly Dressing. The main fly-fishing species in the British Isles are Atlantic salmon, brown trout (sea trout coastally), and European grayling. The instructors are supposed to be knowledgeable on saltwater techniques as well. Ally Gowen, Mark Surtees, and Paul Arden are very active in this organization. Their educational review board is called the AAPGAI Standards and Practices Committee. One thing I did notice, they like to teach one-handed Spey techniques to beginners. The works of "Jock Scott," G.E.M. Skues, Frederick Halford, Frank Sawyer, Fred G. Shaw, Hugh Faulkus, and other English anglers are historic landmarks in the world of fly fishing for salmonid species. They contain some remarkably relevant casting techniques, even by today's standards.

TLT ACADEMY

In 1976 Roberto Pragliola originated the TLT Academy (Technica di Lancio Totale), or translated, Total Technical Launch. In 1987 Roberto was one of the founders of the Italian Fly Fishing School S.I.M. (Scuola Italiana di Pesca a Mosca), and also an EFFA Master Fly-Casting Instructor. In 2010 he founded the TLT Italian Academy of Fly Fishing. The explanation of this technique defies physics, but in practice, I see a specialized technique for brushy stream fishing that works and catches fish. It is claimed to be a stop-less cast and according to Giovanni Nese, TLT Academy, "It uses a system that automatically doubles the speed of the line (reverse hoist) and the vibration of the rod at high frequency according to the third mode of vibration." TLT uses stiff, fast rods like an eight-foot 3-weight with a floater to present dry flies using a long leader, high line speed, and a special grip style. One object is to use low trajectory and high line speed to cause the unrolling loop and leader to land before the belly. This enables the leader to reach under overhangs. I've been told a curve can be made with this technique by making an overpowered curve cast and letting the butt section of the leader land first to unroll in a curve from stored energy. I would think this hard landing would scare wild trout.

When I've watched TLT Instructor Massimo Magliocco, he makes a fast-tempo 170-degree angle side-arm cast with an abundance of wrist motion. He uses a low hand position with the little finger overlapping the reel and the index finger extended partially up the cork. He makes a tight loop this way but I suspect most fishermen would develop wrist muscle fatigue copying it. I consider the dozens of special casts for small streams to be part of the whole picture of fly casting knowledge and TLT offers more tools for us to learn and use.

No one has written as many books and articles on casting or has given as many casting presentations for shows and clubs as Lefty Kreh.

In addition to these organizations, there are many experienced instructors and private schools located all over the globe who are independent and have made significant contributions to our casting technique and learning. Lefty Kreh, IFFF MCI BOG Emeritus, one of the pioneers of saltwater fly fishing whose career spans over fifty years, has written at least ten casting books and many on fly fishing. Lefty has formulated his "Five Principles of Lefty Kreh's Modern Fly Casting Method." Chris Santella wrote in a May 5, 2012, *New York Times* article, "If there is a character in the fly-fishing world who holds rock star cachet, it is Bernard Kreh, better known as Lefty." Gordy has invited Lefty into discussions for his viewpoint in the Master Study Group. Lefty took a long absence from the FFF but was pulled back in by Gordy and fellow BOG member Jim Valle.

Scandinavians have taken Scotland's Spey casts and adapted them for their rocky terrain. Henrik Mortensen of Denmark is one of the most respected instructors of the North who melds techniques together between one- and two-hand systems. His website states he is, "… the inventor of the streamlined ready-to-go shooting heads system …" He worked for *The Loop* at one point and now runs his traveling casting schools and sells his DVD series *Fly Fishing Academy*, and his 2006 book *Flycasting … "The Scandinavian Style."*

Recently, in March 2014, the 9th International Experience of the World of Fly Fishing EWF, was held in Munich, Germany. Representatives from twenty countries and 3600 attendees participated and watched tying and casting demonstrations. Later the same spring, near Hamburg, the German Fly Festival featured experts from fourteen countries with seventy international demonstrators bringing in 700 participants. Alexander Knecht and Bernd Ziesche make up the German Fly Festival organizing team. They are highly qualified and experienced and also operate the First Cast Fly Fishing School.

Roman Moser has been running a casting school and his company, Innovative Fly Fishing Products, for over twenty years in his home in Austria. The Gmundner Traun has been his classroom and product testing ground. Hans Gebetsroither invited him to teach in his fly fishing school while Roman was a local fly tier and was an influence on his casting and fishing.

OUTDOOR INDUSTRY SCHOOLS AND INSTRUCTION

Most independent retail fly shops offer casting lessons using staff for the most part. Most "big-box" retail chain stores offer instruction using guest instructors and others have actual schools for a variety of skills. L.L. Bean Outdoor Discover School offers fly fishing courses at a dozen stores. They also offer casting lessons and preparation for the IFFF Instructor Certifications. I personally know most of their wonderful staff in Freeport, ME, including Rod McGarry, FFF Harger Life Memorial Award recipient, and Macauley Lord, author of the *L.L. Bean Fly Casting Handbook* (2007). He was also the recipient of the FFF Lifetime Achievement Award in 2011.

Orvis Fly Fishing Schools teach all aspects of fly fishing, including casting, in multi-day classes with classrooms and videos at their flagship store in Manchester, VT, plus thirty-three locations nationwide. Tom Rosenbauer is currently the marketing director of Orvis Rod and Tackle and has written over thirty fly fishing books. Whenever and wherever you seek help, asking for the qualifications, experience of the instructors, and referrals, will help you receive quality instruction.

CONCLUSION

In this book I've tried to share ways to be more efficient in your fly casting technique, borrowed from great anglers I've met from around the globe. I've found the difference between average results and excellent results in fly fishing comes from paying attention to small details. Precision and focused efforts make a big difference. I like to cast to feeding fish without my activity affecting their activity. I don't just judge results in numbers of fish or size caught, but by how well I prepared everything and presented my flies. This is an evolution for me, trip by trip, year by year. I hope this book has encouraged you to make learning about our sport and honing your skills a lifetime pursuit. Hopefully, some of my ideas will help prepare you with new fishing strategies for the most challenging situations.

CASTING LINKS

SCHOOLS & INSTRUCTORS

Berne Ziesche Fly Fishing School, Germany
www.first-cast.de/index.html

Henrik Mortensen, Denmark
henrik-mortensen.dk/home

Jason Borger
fishfliesandwater.com

KCS Flycasting School, WA
flycastingmasters.com/marilyn_tony.html

L.L. Bean Fly Fishing Discovery Course
www.llbean.com

Marc Fauvet, France
thelimpcobra.com/fly-casting/

Orvis Fly Fishing Schools
www.orvis.com/fly-fishing-schools

Paul Arden, Sexyloops
www.sexyloops.com/flycasting/contents.shtml

Peter Hayes, Tasmania
www.peterhayesflyfishing.com/default.aspx

TLT Academy-Italy
www.tltacademy.it

Wulff School of Fly Fishing
wulffschool.com

CLUBS & ORGANIZATIONS

AAPGAI
www.aapgai.co.uk

American Casting Association
www.americancastingassoc.org

EFFA
www.effa.info/startseite.187.html

Flycasting National Committee of Spain
comisionnacionaldelanzado.blogspot.com

GGACC, San Francisco, CA
www.ggacc.org

IFFF
www.fedflyfishers.org

Long Beach Casting Club, CA
www.longbeachcastingclub.org
Royal Casting Club De Belgique
www.pechemouche.be
The Oakland Casting Club, Oakland, CA
oaklandcastingclub.org
World Championship in Flycasting
www.wcflycasting.com

ACKNOWLEDGEMENTS

I would like to acknowledge and thank the following organizations and individuals for their expertise, inspiration, contributions, and assistance in this book; the International Federation of Fly Fishers, American Casting Association, the Master Study Group (moderated by Gordy Hill), Macauley Lord, Gordy Hill, Tom White, Jason Borger, Chris Korich, Nick Lyons, Jay Cassell, Jonathan McCullough, Paul Arden, Dick Fujita, Bob Jacklin, Bill Keister, Ellis Newman, Hap Heins, Bruce Chard, Henry Mittel, Steve Rajeff, Tim Rajeff, Alan Gnann, Bruce Richards, Joan Wulff, Ted Rogowski, Jim Krul, Chris Theising, Per Brandin, James Anderson and The Yellowstone Angler, The Compleat Angler, Charles Jardine, Kevney Moses, Jim Valle, Jim Krul, and last but not least, my wife Edina and children, Dylan and Stephanie.

GLOSSARY

Annular sector: a four-sided shape described by two radii and two concentric arcs. I use it to describe the path within the stroke and the rod arc.

Casting fault: An action or inaction that has a negative affect on an intended cast.

Casting stroke: the path the hand takes during a cast.

CI: Casting Instructor—IFFF Certified

Creep: The unintentional forward or backward rod-hand movement, before loading the rod.

Drag: Intentional forward or backward rod-hand movement, before loading the rod used to eliminate slack.

Drift: Intentional rearward repositioning of the rod after loop formation of the backcast.

Line diameter and lb. test formulas:

$$11 - \underline{} \text{ dia.} = \underline{} X$$
$$11 - \underline{} X = \underline{} \text{ dia.}$$
$$9 - \underline{} X = \underline{} \text{ lb. test}$$

Loop: In the words of Bruce Richards, "The shape of an aerialized fly line formed by a casting stroke." Or the "J" shape of a fly line after it has been made airborne by a casting stroke or snap and then sharply decelerated.

MCI: Master Casting Instructor—IFFF Certified

Rod plane: The planar path of a rod during a cast.

Rod angle: The angle of a rod at a given time in relation to vertical and to the direction of the cast.

Rod arc: The change in rod butt angle from the beginning of rod loading to unloading.

Rod loading: The act of bending the rod by using making a casting stroke.

Rod stop: A term used to describe the rapid deceleration of a fly line. Since there is some inertia and flex in an outfit casting line, the stop does not occur instantaneously like a single handclap.

Rod-tip path: The path traveled by the rod tip during a cast.

Rotation: The angular movement of the rod butt caused by the rod hand.

Rule of 30: 30 x line weight= grains

THCI: Two Hand Casting Instructor—IFFF Certified

Translation: Horizontal movement of the rod butt without a change in rod butt angle.

BIBLIOGRAPHY

My Angling Friends, Fred Mather, Forest and Stream, 1901, p.110.

Where Anglers Rear Back and Let Fly, New York Times, James Card. August 9th, 2010.

The Talent Code, Bantam, Daniel Coyle, 2009.

"Six-Step Approach to Casting Faults and Cures" which was published in the Spring 1999 Issue of *The Loop Newsletter*, IFFF.

Casting and Fishing the Artificial Fly, Caxton Printers Ltd., John W. Ball, 1972, p.63 (Fig.8) "Movement of Casting Hand.".

The Essentials of Fly Casting, Federation of Fly Fishers, Bill Gammill, 1993.

Modern Fly Casting Method, Lyons Press, Lefty Kreh 2003, p. 137.

Troubleshooting the Cast, Stackpole Books, Ed Jaworawski 1999, p.17.

A River Runs through It, University of Chicago Press. Norman MacLean 1976 p. 4.

"*Mooch*" The Creel 9, Tom McAlister, ACA? (Dec 1971 p.18-21).

George Cook on *Spey Casting Secrets*, Native Fish Society, 2003.

Corkscrew Curve Cast, (article) Fly Fisherman Magazine May/June 1980, Gary A. Borger and Bob Petzl.

Flycasting Accuracy, Fall 2007 Issue, IFFF The Loop, Larry Allen, p.25.

Atlantic Salmon Magic, Wild River Press, Topher Browne 2011 p.119-123.

Trout Fishing Techniques, Lyons & Burford, John Goddard,1996 p.85.

Under the Wind, Spring 2001, The Loop, Larry Pratt PhD p.1.

The Complete Science of Fly Fishing and Spinning, by Frederick G. Shaw, London, 1915 p. 181.

Slack Line Strategies for Fly Fishing, Stackpole, John Judy 1994.

Nature of Fly Casting, Shadow Caster Press, Jason Borger 2001 p.233.

Nymphs and the Trout, Stanley Paul, Frank Sawyer 1958 p. 98-99.

Techniques of Trout Fishing and Fly Tying, Lyons & Burford, George W. Harvey 1990 p. 44.

Slack Line Strategies for Fly Fishing, Stackpole, John Judy 1994 p.61.

Vol. I *Fishing, Salmon and Trout*, Badminton Library of Sports and Pastimes, H. Cholmonde-ley-Pennell, 1885 p. 226-228.

Modern Fly Casting, Charles Scribner's Sons, John Alden Knight, 1942.

Slack Line Strategies for Fly Fishing, Stackpole, John Judy 1994 p.61.

Fly Casting for Salmon, Fishing with the fly: Sketches by lovers of the art, Edited by Charles F. Orvis George Dawson 1883.

Sport Mechanics for Coaches, 3rd Edition, Brendan Burkett BEng, MEng, PhD Human Kinetics, 2010.

Harvey Pennic, "Find the best (caster) in the world and copy their style but only do so if you are built like them."

In the Ring of the Rise, The Lyons Press, Vincent C. Marinaro, 2001, p.39.

The Essence of Flycasting II, (video) Krieger Enterprises, Mel Krieger 2003.

"eight rods—eight casters: test of five line rods" online at Sexyloops.com.

Fly Fishing the Harriman Ranch, Whitefish Press, John McDaniel, 2012 p.76.

The Technology of Fly Rods, Frank Amato Publications, Don Phillips, 2000 pp.44-45.

How Does Stretch Affect the Cast`Lesson in Timelessness by a Fly-Fishing Master, New York Times, May 5th 2012, Chris Santella.

INDEX